THEY'LL NEVER BELIEVE ME!

THEY'LL NEVER BELIEVE ME!

Elsie Pilling

JANUS PUBLISHING COMPANY
London, England

First published in Great Britain 1996
by Janus Publishing Company,
Edinburgh House, 19 Nassau Street,
London W1N 7RE

Copyright © Elsie Pilling 1996

**British Library Cataloguing-in-Publication Data.
A catalogue record for this book is available from the
British Library.**

ISBN 1 85756 271 2

All rights reserved. No part of this publication may be
reproduced, stored in a retrieval system or transmitted in
any form or by any means, electronic, mechanical,
photocopying, recording or otherwise, without the prior
permission of the publisher.

The right of Elsie Pilling to be identified
as the author of this work has been asserted by her
in accordance with the Copyright, Designs and Patents
Act 1988.

Cover design Harold King
Printed & bound in England by
Antony Rowe Ltd,
Chippenham, Wiltshire

ACKNOWLEDGEMENTS

NONE OF THE characters in this book are fictitious but all have pseudonyms. I am deeply grateful to each of them for being the kind of people worth writing about and to most of them for having coloured a large portion of my life.

To my family – husband Eddie, son Michael and daughter Karen – my thanks for initial encouragement extending into many years of patience, tolerance and endurance. To Walter Nash, Professor Emeritus of Nottingham University, I extend grateful thanks for his invaluable help with the technicalities of transforming sheets of second-rate typing into grist for a publisher.

FOREWORD

WHAT MOTIVATES A person to write a book? Allow me to speak for myself since I am entirely unqualified to speak for any other person.

Picture, if you will, a 'run-of-the-mill' seven-year-old elevated into raptures of delight on receiving twenty out of twenty for Composition. At this point, I feel it necessary to explain, for the edification of members of a younger generation, that composition was the name given to that exercise presently known as creative writing. Modesty does not prevent me revealing that I continued to receive consistently high marks throughout the rest of my junior school career blossoming, during grammar school and college life, into 'As' or 'Bs' when compositions were known under more distinguished designation as 'essays'. In the years following those halcyon student days, my writing has consisted of lengthy letters to friends and relatives; composition of semi-humorous verse celebrating important events in the life of the family and the occasional letter to the local press. I enjoy writing. Many people have exhorted me to go into print in a big way – 'You really ought to write a book!'

Being a parson's wife, mother and full-time teacher tended to limit my writing to necessary correspondence and matters of administration but recent early retirement, the presentation of a portable typewriter and the loan of a 'Teach Yourself to Type' manual puts a different complexion on the matter. Could it be that writing is my God-given talent to be spread beyond the bound of family and friends? This book is concerned with some of my experiences as a teacher. I would wish it to dissipate gloom and despondency but, also, to stir rebellion against flagrant injustice wrapped in the mantle of authority.

CHAPTER ONE

'SHE'LL BE A teacher when she grows up!' The very first time I recall hearing that proclamation was whilst I was engaged upon a very serious exercise. As conductor of our infant school percussion band, I was endeavouring, with all the expertise of a six-year-old, to guide my classmates through the intricacies of the tonic sol-fa, sorting out the 'fahs' from the 'sohs'. Try telling that to the youth of today! Not only will they refuse to believe you, they won't have the faintest idea what you're talking about. We were in rehearsal for the major event of our school year – the visit of the mayor and part of his corporation! The percussion band was the *pièce de résistance* of the infant department. Staff of the junior school and the headmaster himself – awesome personage – had come along to hear our cacophany and, I suspect, to decide whether or not it would be acceptable to His Worship's auditory senses. I've no doubt that the prophetic utterance regarding my future career was highly complimentary coming, as it did, from one who was already a member of that august profession. Its effect on me was so shattering that only my highly developed power of self-control prevented the band from collapsing into a complete shambles.

I must confess that I hadn't given too much thought to my future career but a teacher was just about the last thing I would have thought of becoming. Teachers were old people who made you do things you didn't want to do, shouted at you when you did them and slapped your legs when you didn't. Teachers had their priorities wrong. When

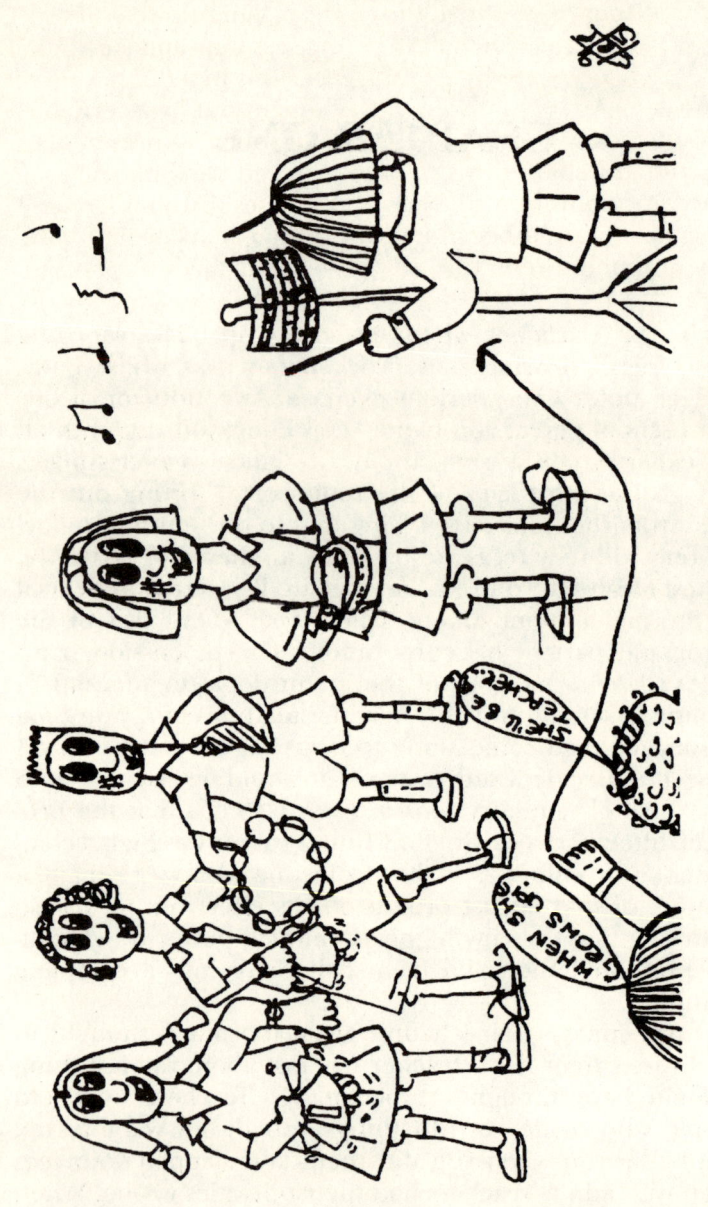

The Percussion Band – drawn by Clare & Rachel Pilling

I decided to go into the countryside picking flowers, listening to bird song and benefiting from fresh air and sunshine in preference to coping with difficult sums in a dingy, musty classroom – what happened? I was sought out by a veritable posse including the dreaded 'school bobby' – present-day educational welfare officer – and dragged back into school to face an inquisition of 'Sirs' and 'Misses'. Administration of the cane, waived because of my tender years, would have been infinitely preferable to those stern faces and harsh voices that reduced a sensitive, nature-loving, affectionate child into a cringing, trembling wreck of humanity. Join such as them! The mere idea was abhorrent to my six-year-old mind. 'I'll never be a teacher,' I said to myself.

Time passed and, as the infant blossomed through standards one, two and three, she continued to develop a positive anti-teacher complex. My mother was always a most hospitable creature and was never happier than when the table was fully extended to accommodate as many potential diners as possible and bearing a load proving, beyond any shadow of a doubt, that table legs were 'better made then than what they are now'. I learnt to accommodate myself to all sorts and conditions of men and women for my parents made no distinction between rich and poor; intelligent or of inferior mentality; professional or unskilled; influential or of little account by worldly standard. A weaver might be seated on my left, a managing director on my right, whilst, sitting opposite, happily masticating the diverse ingredients of the inevitable ham salad, would be the editor of the local newspaper passing the condiments to the wife of the local coalman. Though I sometimes resented missing Uncle Mac or Romany – try telling that to the youth of today! – my healthy appetite appreciated the more than usually lavish spread except on those occasions when one of the company happened to be a teacher! Then, the cream-horns turned sour, the strawberries became revoltingly acidic and my happy, childish prattling came to an abrupt halt. My beloved parents seemed such eminently sensible people but how could any sensible person ask a teacher to tea? There couldn't be many people who'd invite a teacher to tea! '*I'm not going to be a teacher,*' I said to myself.

Naturally enough, I passed the eleven-plus – what else can you do when so many people are misguidedly convinced that teaching is your ultimate vocation? Even an eleven-plus-year-old knows that you've to be clever in order to develop those dastardly traits whereby you make a child sufficiently malleable to be responsive to your fiendish control and crafty manipulation.

After a few weeks of settling-in at the municipal high school, I decided that members of staff in this educational establishment were a different kettle of fish altogether. Apart from two teachers who'd taught my mother and only just missed my father, they seemed to be a comparatively youthful set. I was smitten by an extremely attractive PE mistress and a handsomely debonair English master and fancied the emotion to be reciprocated but believe, in retrospect, that my intense interest in their respective subjects was the reason for their friendly attention. That would also account for the fact that the art master – recipient of innumerable schoolgirl 'pashes' – left my emotions completely unruffled.

It was unfortunate that my first year at grammar school (youngsters should make the most of them while they're still around) coincided with the commencement of hostilities or, to put it in a less refined manner, the year war broke out. Just as my anti-teacher complex was beginning to melt around the edges, young teachers departed to serve King and country and were replaced by more mature members of the profession and, eventually, by several brought out of retirement. It would be ungracious of me to continue further without acknowledging a debt of gratitude to the numerous teachers who gave me knowledge and 'know-how' throughout the impressionable years of adolescence. 'Distance lends enchantment' but they weren't a bad bunch on the whole!

As the war that was going to be over by the Christmas of 1939 rolled into its fifth year, I attained the exalted position of prefect. Through my attempts to deal firmly, but justly, with unruly individuals of the lower fifth there came, yet again, the now familiar prophecy: 'She's going to be a teacher'. This time my denial was definitely less emphatic. Two of my cousins were officers in the WRNS and looked a knock-out in their uniforms. For entirely the wrong reasons, I was strongly attracted to following in their footsteps but had a feeling that present hostilities would have ceased before I became old enough to serve in HM Forces. I was in the sixth form and, in those days, the few entrants to the 'sixth' had, generally speaking, three choices of career open to them: doctor, teacher or parson. A prospective doctor required, as is still the case, qualifications on the science side and science was definitely not my forte. Females were ineligible to train for the ministry – and still are in certain denominations! By a simple process of elimination it looked as if I was going to be a teacher, so giving numerous individuals the satisfaction of saying 'I told you so!'

Though feeling somewhat chagrined in my acquiescence to the 'prophets', I began to give serious consideration to this idea of becoming an educator of children. Being a teacher brought with it an automatic prestige and status level! A teacher's signature was legitimately acceptable as a witness on highly important official documents, in fact, for such purposes, a teacher was on a par with JPs, GPs and even MPs! Having been in school for twelve years, I was fully aware that a teacher's job was a 'doddle'. Seven hours a day, including lunch breaks, dinner breaks and free periods; long and frequent holidays; the only exertion that of carrying books from one room to another, giving orders, scrawling suitably impressive comments on exercise books and pupils' annual reports and, occasionally, supervising after-school detention. The more I thought about it, the more I wondered why anyone ever considered being anything other than a teacher and I said to myself:-

'I'M GOING TO BE A TEACHER!'

Having made the first big decision I was confronted by the second – what sort of a teacher? Thoughts of myself as a winsome and popular PE mistress were rapidly dispelled when a friend intimated that over-developed muscles, relatively attractive in early life, would turn into unsightly flab during years of greater maturity. My Headmaster was convinced that, for his Head Girl, nothing less than a place at one of the well established and highly prestigious universities could be considered – good copy for the local press and a boost for the reputation of the school! Many heads of today cherish similar aspirations. Four years of higher education was completely out of my reckoning. Hadn't I decided, years earlier, that I would be married at the age of twenty-three and, thereafter, having paid my debt to society, be kept in the manner to which I'd been accustomed (if not better!). Two years at a teacher training college – known now as 'colleges of education' and with a minimum three-year course – would adequately suit my purpose. Such proved to be the case and, after an enjoyable and eventful training period, I emerged. I was a teacher and had a certificate to prove it.

I WAS A TEACHER!!

CHAPTER TWO

ALTHOUGH MY TWO years in college and my twelve weeks of teaching practice had been concerned with the education of children in the secondary modern school, I was allocated to a junior school. The Director of Education had been sufficiently courteous as to consult my feelings upon the matter – such is not always the case in this day and age! He also explained the reason. I wasn't the only one to have emerged as a teacher in that year of 1947. A large number of men, newly demobbed from HM Forces, had elected to undergo a twelve-month period of emergency training and were now expressing a preference for placement in secondary schools. Who was I to stand in their way? They had spent less time at college than I had but years spent in serving their country had given them a comprehensive education in the university of life and, despite adverse murmurings from numbers of well-established teachers, I felt them to be better equipped than most for the responsible task of educating adolescent minds. So it was that I stood one day in a slum-clearance area of a Lancashire cotton town gazing at the dirty, decrepit junior school building with four none-too-steady walls, where I was to begin my long-forecast career. Taking my courage in both hands and wondering why I'd ever been persuaded into becoming a teacher, I went inside to meet the Headmaster, future colleagues and the children who were about to be entrusted to my care.

The school building was old; the furnishings sparsely utilitarian; equipment scarce and staff-room non-existent. Those teachers not involved in playground duty met together at 'break' in the none-purpose-designed kitchen and sat on hard chairs round an ammonia-scrubbed, wooden-topped table. Partitioned classrooms surrounded three sides of the hall and one side of two entrance corridors. Each classroom was packed to near capacity with ancient, heavy desks and ancient, heavy chairs and ancient heavy cupboards filled with ancient, heavy books. Outside my classroom was the playground – an area of uneven flagstones hemmed in, on two sides, by a high wall of disintegrating, dingy brickwork. Opposite my classroom window and running parallel to it, was the toilet accommodation which, when not flooded with rainwater was still flooded (if you get my drift!) and from which wafted odious vapours, particularly when the wind was in a certain quarter. The one staff toilet was situated 'across t' playground', access being gained by means of a large, warder-type key usually suspended from a hook firmly screwed into the wooden partition of staff-room-cum-non-purpose-built kitchen.

One Headmaster, Mr Johnson, eight staff members, one cheerful and efficient caretaker and three hundred children populated this grim edifice whose seemingly sole recommendation was that it was on the level (factually, if not always figuratively speaking). If stone walls do not a prison make, neither do they make a school. The personality and expertise of those who work within the stone walls make the school and ours was a 'good 'un'. We were known as a 'scholarship school' and it was a pride and joy to us that several of 'our' children gained entrance to Manchester Grammar School as well as to the more local grammar schools. Far more important, we were a happy school – a school in which the children of professional people literally rubbed shoulders with children of jailbirds and prostitutes; a school in which the staff were happy and friendly, caring for one another and for the children they taught. Ours was a rough school and I came to know many members of the local constabulary. Though rough, it was also ready and I soon felt thoroughly at home within the building that had filled me with initial apprehension.

With my first year of teaching came my twenty-first birthday but I had no reason to suspect that the fact would be known in my place of employment. Imagine my surprise when, after morning prayers on that auspicious day, the assembled company sang Happy Birthday following the enthusiastic, if somewhat untuneful, rendering by a roof-raising three cheers. Our school roof was eminently raiseable. Whenever rain fell, a not infrequent occurrence in Rochdale, children were despatched to place dozens of buckets in strategic places and we were subjected to the Chinese type torture of the regular drip! To get back to the birthday. Surprises continued within the relative privacy of the classroom as several children made individual presentations. Among the latter was a magnificent birthday cake baked by a master confectioner of the town whose daughter was, happily, one of my pupils. As I was about to mark the register at the beginning of the afternoon session, two of my roughest, toughest lads staggered through the classroom door. The cause of their staggering was an obviously heavy load concealed in layers of newsprint. Having laid down their burden, wiped their respective noses on the backs of their respective hands and paused to draw breath, they delivered their oration: 'It's for you, Miss.'

I began to peel off the wrapping paper. As I did so, the grime on the donors' faces was enhanced by their beams of proud benevolence. Then came the moment of revelation amid the 'Oohs' and 'Ahs' of excited children. There, upon my desk, stood a magnificent bronze statuette depicting a rearing horse surmounted by a rider whose alarmed expression was akin to mine as I recognised the gift as identical to an *objet d'art* usually gracing the front window of a nearby house. Pulling myself together and remembering 'it's the thought that counts' and 'one should never look a gift-horse in the mouth', I warmed the hearts of two well-meaning criminals by ardent expressions of gratitude whilst keeping a sharp look-out for my friends of the plain-clothes branch. The latter listened patiently to my plea of extenuating circumstances and reinforced my faith in the good old

The bronze statuette – drawn by Ron Standring

British Bobby. Two miscreants escaped with a firm but kindly caution; the statuette was returned to its forgiving owners and I accepted a grubby packet of chewing-gum in lieu of the bronze casting. 'The road to Hell is paved with good intentions.'

I was less amicably disposed to the young arsonist whose intentions were anything but good! Bobby had been sent from London to live with his grandparents in the hope that they might be able to exercise the control that his parents had failed to give. His school record made appalling reading and it was hardly surprising that I was repeatedly questioned, by Mr Johnson and colleagues, concerning Bobby's behaviour in my classroom. Hadn't I always known, in my heart of hearts, that teaching was my vocation! Bobby's behaviour was impeccable. He buckled down to his work in a most helpful and cooperative manner and, after a few weeks, I began 'to take my eyes off him'. Was I not succeeding where others, in a far more exalted and experienced position than me, had failed! 'Pride cometh just before the fall' and, on a never to be forgotten day, thick smoke began to rise from the close proximity of Bobby's desk. As leaping flames followed the smoke, children were evacuated. Dinner ladies formed themselves into a human chain of water-filled jug passers and the conflagration was soon under control.

Bobby had lulled me into a sense of false security. The scheming little lad had asked for a desk by the window so that he could utilise the maximum of light whilst engaged in his academic pursuits. It was no coincidence that a large ventilation grille nestled in the wall alongside his position. During recurring short periods when he'd been, to all intents and purposes, extracting worn pen nibs by use of his shoe heel, he'd also been engaged in prising up a floor-board and filling the resultant cavity with dry tinder. Choosing a day when a strong wind whistled freely through the grille, he'd dropped his lighted match. Bobby was removed from our school forthwith and placed, no doubt, with people less gullible than myself. So much for my expertise in child psychology and so much for my 96% in the theory of that subject! I know what it is to fall from a pedestal upon which one should never have climbed in the first place!

The reference to child psychology reminds me of yet another case-history. Paul was a grand little lad. When it was suggested that he was involved in nefarious exercises, I just knew myself to be correct in protesting his innocence. Hadn't I proved the trustworthiness of 'my' children by leaving a valuable, ivory-trimmed penknife unguardedly in evidence and finding it in exactly the same position whenever I returned to the classroom after unavoidable absence? To return to Paul. A more honest, open, dependable child you'd go a long way to find – always providing you were motivated to do so. He was the sort of child who must have inspired St Augustine to remark – 'Not Angles but angels!' A rosy-cheeked, blue-eyed, golden-haired boy, thoroughly amenable to discipline and a pleasure to have in the classroom. In short, Paul was the delight of a teacher's life! When it was suggested that I should surreptitiously follow this model of perfection as he wended his way homeward, I actually entered into argument with a member of the constabulary suggesting that such sleuthing tactics came more within his province than mine. Eventually, believing the information that Paul could 'smell' an officer of the law a mile away and, incidentally, wondering what might befall a young lady refusing to cooperate, I declared myself willing to adopt this Sherlock Holmes-type role. It would make a change from teaching, might be quite exciting and would certainly put me in a position to exonerate my pupil from whatever heinous crime he was suspected of perpetrating.

Paul, largely due to his efficiency and gentle demeanour, was one of my envied monitors so there was no suspicion as to my motives when he was requested to stay behind one afternoon and tidy the classroom. As he took his coat from one of many pegs in the boys' cloakroom, I was hiding behind the outer door and, when he left the school premises I padded, softly and silently, in his wake. At this point, I would advise readers who suffer a tendency to heightened blood pressure to skip the next few lines – the tension could be catastrophic! So we continued, Paul and his shadow, through the dusky alleyways of that Lancashire town, until, at last, we emerged into the brightness of the main shopping area. Paul disappeared into a large store, reappearing so quickly that, had I not been so adept in the art of dodging – I hadn't been centre-attack in the school netball team for nothing! – we would surely have been involved in a head-on collision. His pace accelerated and he seemed to have developed a distinct swelling of the right hip-joint. Back into the murky side streets we sped and I was grateful for my experience as right wing in the first eleven of the high school hockey team. When Paul came to a halt beside the rickety gate of a partially demolished house, he wasn't just pausing to draw breath. He lifted a gatepost out of its socket, dropped something into it, replaced the post and continued on his way.

Ten minutes later a subdued and breathless teacher reported at the police station. Paul was in the employ of a Fagin-like father who knew the inside of a prison better than he knew the outside! The actual theft of the goods – a camera on this occasion – was imposed upon the lad by a man who later collected and profitably disposed of them. Paul's reward was an escape from the belting promised for non-production of loot! 'The iniquities of the fathers shall be visited upon the sons.'

One winter afternoon, I decided to stay at school to mark some books in preference to carrying them home on the seven-mile bus journey. Taking a short cut into the town, *en route* to the bus terminus, I noticed a group of children gathered around a bonfire on a piece of waste ground. An innocent, if potentially dangerous, pastime I thought, as I made my way towards them. Suddenly I was frozen to the spot by a spine-chilling, inhuman, unrecognisable sound. Aware of my approaching presence, the children scattered, leaving me to gaze helplessly as a cat expired in the glowing embers of the fire. Research revealed a pair of bloodstained shears lying on the ground. The children hadn't escaped sufficiently quickly to prevent me recognising familiar faces and those faces, attached to respective bodies, appeared before Mr Johnson the following morning. They'd only been disturbed playing one of their favourite games in which they caught a cat, profuse among the dereliction of that slum-clearance area, cut off its tail with shears sharpened by the son of the owners of a well-known hardware store and, finally, roasted the skewered animal until death ended its horrendous ordeal. Those were the days when corporal punishment was seen as the ultimate deterrent and the torturers were tortured, to a far lesser degree than their victims, in the presence of their schoolmates. The lesson was salutary and the feline inhabitants of the district gained a reprieve which remained effective during the rest of my career in that area and, I dare to hope, is effective forty years later.

In the 1990s we are concerned – and rightly so – about the deplorable behaviour of some of our children but let us beware suggesting that this is an entirely novel phenomenon and let us be concerned to ensure that an effective deterrent is available to the teachers of today.

CHAPTER THREE

A SENSE OF humour is surely one of the best of God's gifts. It's certainly one of the things I prize and without which my life would have been much less colourful and infinitely less happy.

Most members of my profession must have spent many happy hours in laughing at the contents of certain letters from certain parents. Please don't misunderstand me and be not quick to take offence, ye parent-readers! I myself, am a parent of considerable experience and am quick to leap to our defence when we're under attack from childless, 'know-it-all' members of staff but, honestly, some of your letters are a scream and brighten our existence. Carry on writing!

I recall one occasion when a brief letter – more of a note really – caused me anything but hilarity. 'Barbara can't cum to school has she, as scarlet fever.' 'So what?' you may be saying to yourself if you're under thirty years of age (or pretending to be). 'So a great deal!' would be my reply. In my days as a very young teacher, scarlet fever was still a disease which struck fear into the heart and called for immediate action. The relevant health authority was speedily informed. My classroom was invaded by masked men and women freely squirting – without so much as a 'by your leave' – evil-smelling disinfectant over desks and chairs, children and teacher and gathering together, with carefully gloved hands, Barbara's school books prior to burning them. I was alerted to the symptoms heralding the onslaught of this potentially fatal disease and my ever fertile imagination began to run riot. Two days later, Barbara walked nonchalantly into the classroom. 'I thought you had scarlet fever!' came my tremulous cry. 'Please Miss Standring, mi mum couldn't spell diarrhoea,' was her down-to-earth reply. Can *you* spell that debilitating complaint without reference to a dictionary? Wouldn't you have had the sense to substitute 'the common cold' in preference to the dreaded scarlet fever?

In those post-war days, when ration books were still the order of the day, we were very conscious of the adage 'Waste not, want not'. Those of us brought up under wartime conditions are still to be found scraping the butter off the bread rather than putting it on! With that in mind, you will appreciate the consternation caused when free milk was not being consumed by each and every child and full bottles were to be found in the crates at the end of a school day. Mr Johnson decided that each child would be forcibly fed (or milked!) unless he or she brought an acceptable note from Mum or Dad. The words of one of these notes are indelibly fixed in my mind and are about to be put down on paper for the second time: 'Janet honly drinks milk what cums from cows not that what cums from bockles.' There's an answer to that but we teachers are encouraged to be constructive and must give parents the benefit of the doubt, so to speak. I've frequently wondered from whence Janet's parents assumed bottled milk came. The mind boggles! Many more amusing parental letters spring to mind but, leaving you with those two gems, I'll proceed with amusing incidents unrelated to the written word.

'Music and movement' – an accepted event in present-day primary schools – was a novelty on my entry into the teaching profession. The children and I loved it. I would do a quick-change act behind the blackboard and emerge in the full splendour of my not-unattractive young womanhood wearing daring PE shorts that were at least eighteen inches above my knees. It was surprising how many male teachers found it necessary to cross the hall during our movement lessons and not at all surprising that Mr Johnson found it expedient to interest himself in this particular activity – was it not his job to familiarise himself with new programmes and assess their efficiency?

For those unfamiliar with this aforementioned schools' radio programme, a word of information. Music and movement involves moving to music in a free, imaginative and creative manner and has been known to produce near-riots though not, I hasten to add, in any of my well organised classes. I can't tell you the things into which I've been transformed during sessions of this enervating exercise. The list is endless including such objects, as animals, various giants, sea-shells, astronauts, waves, breezes, vehicles, snakes, etc. etc. I well remember a particular day when, along with the children, I had become a tree. At first the forty or so trees swayed gently in a whispering breeze but rapidly increasing velocity resulted in an ultimate buffeting by severe gale-force winds. As my trunk groaned and my branches became frenzied appendages, I took time to wave one of them to one of my constabulary friends as he approached my Headmaster. At the time, I thought the wild look in the eye of the latter to be due to the turbulent atmosphere created by our gyrations but learnt later that he'd been trying to convey the fact that the supposed police officer was none other than the Director of Education. Not in my wildest dreams would I have dared to project an image of myself as a creaking branch in the presence of my Director. I blush at the recollection of one of my most embarrassing moments. Relief came when Mr Johnson assured me that the Director had been most impressed by the lesson he'd witnessed. It would have been a hard man indeed who could have remained unmoved by such a creative demonstration and he could consider himself fortunate to have escaped the full force of the near-hurricane. 'I don't know what you'll do next lass' – my father's words ring in my ears.

Most teachers will have experienced the purposeful approach of a seemingly belligerent parent and performed a rapid mental run-down on confiscated toys and/or smacked

Waving the creaking branch – drawn by Ron Standring

bottoms before assuming a blandly innocent and thoroughly welcoming attitude. When the classroom door bursts open and a guttural voice demands to know why you've administered corporal punishment to 'our John' then a prompt and comprehensive explanation is the order of the day. Putting down the child held suspended by the scruff of its neck and fixing the rest of the children with your 'titter if you dare' expression, you make a rapid decision as to which of your four Johns is the subject in question. Being a teacher whose 'laying-on-of-hands' is relatively infrequent, I had little difficulty in isolating the particular child nor, indeed, of recalling his crime. To say that John had a colourful vocabulary would be misleading but to say that he was in the habit of prefacing every noun by an adjective that gave it a definite reddish hue would be entirely correct.

I had explained to the class as a whole, and to John in particular, that the adjective was legitimate in certain circumstances but that, when used illegitimately, it became a swear word and was thus beyond the bounds of classroom useage. Those weren't the exact words used but such was the meaning behind them. John persisted in wearing his rose-coloured spectacles until, in sheer exasperation, I threatened that, if the offending word fell from his lips once more, my hand would fall upon a certain fleshy portion of his anatomy. Every good teacher knows, as every good parent should, that a promised threat is useless if not put into action. The next time John's words became bloodshot his fleshy thighs came out in sympathy.

All this I explained, simply and briefly, to John's dad. The latter applauded my action remarking that he didn't know where his son picked up this b... swearing but if he b... well swore again I could b... well give him another b... smack and he wouldn't b... well interfere. It must be true that people whose every other spoken word is a swear word just don't realise that they *are* swearing. Language aside, John's dad and I were allies from that day forth and, when a man's over six feet in height and of impressive shoulder span, it's diplomatic to keep things that way. 'Discretion is the better part of valour.'

CHAPTER FOUR

As an assistant teacher, one's immediate authority is the head-teacher. Head-teachers are of both sexes and come in varying shapes and sizes. In my younger days, they were invariably people who'd had considerable experience in teaching and knew how to relate to adults as well as to children. My first 'Head' was of the male species and middle-aged both in years and outlook. He was of average height, stocky in build, grey-haired, good humoured and a loveable rascal. 'We kill or cure at this school,' he said. 'If they're swimmin' we leave 'em alone, if they're sinkin' we jump in and pull 'em out.' As no one came to pull me out during those five years I assume that I was a swimmer, of sorts.

I looked upon Mr Johnson as a father-figure. His staff comprised three middle-aged women and a middle-aged man who were his contemporaries (two of them had been in the same class at junior school); two emergency-trained men who hadn't opted for senior school teaching; one typical school-ma'am of indeterminate age, and me. Hardly surprising that I should be looked upon as a daughter and be the recipient of affectionate squeezes! He was a good head, exercising firm but kindly discipline, but he was human and, like all humans, he had his faults. During coffee breaks and dinner hours he would submit to good-humoured banter from former classmates. 'Come off it, Arnold' they'd say if he attempted to usurp his authority or 'Pull the other one' on occasions when his imagination tended to run riot. In spite of such banter, there was great loyalty to a Head concerned for the well-being of staff and children. We laughed about the number of 'close' relatives whose regular deceases provided a day's absence, with pay. We laughed about the weekly letter, surreptitiously slid from kitchen table into trilby hat, from a certain female student at a Lakeland training college, a young lady introduced to us, on her visits during 'vacs', as a friend of the family but whom we strongly suspected to be no friend of Mrs Johnson! Our affection for this rogue, enjoying his second childhood like a mischievous schoolboy, precluded any idea of splitting on him. We displayed the tolerance of Dutch uncles.

The attitude of a head-teacher can make or mar the life of an assistant teacher, especially one just beginning his or her career and very liable to make many mistakes. I have cause to be grateful to Mr Johnson. After a period of three years at his school, I intended to apply for a position on the staff of a school for 'backward' children shortly to be opened in the premises of my home church. Mr Johnson was more than generous in the testimonial he wrote for me. Among other things, he stated how very sorry he would be to lose my services. I withdrew my application. Since that time, I have learnt that certain head-teachers are in the habit of providing glowing references for those of their staff who have become 'thorns in the flesh'. May I, therefore, take this opportunity of apologising to an extremely elderly Mr Johnson, who may be still in the land of the living, for thwarting his intentions of forty-odd years ago. 'The best laid plans o' mice and men gang aft agley.'

In authority over the head-teacher is a magnificent array of personnel, some responsible to the local director of education and others to the Ministry of Education. Titles vary greatly and mean little to the layman and not a deal more to the professional! We must remember that 'A rose, by any other name, would smell as sweet.' One of the male species of titled authority took it upon himself (or was directed by his director) to take me under his wing, figuratively speaking, during the first months of my teaching career.

If his intention was to be of help then he failed miserably. His poker-faced domineering attitude filled me with a terror that is, in retrospect, almost unbelievable. Even today, when advisors advise in a helpful and sympathetic manner, young colleagues are still reduced to a state of knee-wobbling trepidation at the prospect of a visit. Imagine then the condition of *my* nervous system! Mr Evans would bluster into my classroom, pushing children roughly and rudely out of his way, and proceed to establish himself in a conspicuous position. My dialogue was frequently interrupted by scathingly sarcastic comments. He deprecated the dulcet tone of my voice, constantly reiterating that I should be capable of being heard on the main road some three hundred yards distant. To my mind, there were at least two factors against such an objective. Firstly, I wasn't teaching people who were travelling along the main road and, secondly, I was in a partition classroom and in competition with the teacher next door. When I summoned the temerity to express my doubts concerning voice production, he demonstrated the stridency of his own vocal expertise in such a way as to bring several colleagues rushing to my assistance.

On account of his far from tender ministrations, I spent sleepless nights crying into my pillow. Vainly I tried to follow the advice of my Headmaster: 'Agree with his suggestions and then forget 'em and carry on as though you'd never 'eard 'em.' After six months of intermittent visiting, Mr Evans reported very favourably on my potential as an asset to the educational world. His report did nothing to compensate for my six months of agonising. There are still individuals in the world of education who cherish a Draculean image, delighting in reducing their subordinates to cringing inability – may God forgive them more readily than I feel able to do.

Bouncing into school one day, during my second year of teaching, came a member of Her Majesty's inspectorate, an exponent of free discipline and an example of the same! Miss Fannakerpan, which seems as good a name as any for one of the scattiest individuals I've ever met, reminded me of that wonderful actress Joyce Grenfell in her role as an extrovert PE mistress. Under the influence of this HMI the most reliable of children became remarkably unstable whilst those potentially unstable became hopelessly out of control. 'Suppose we all become busy little bees,' said Miss Fannakerpan as I gave up on a well-planned nature lesson. The children began to flap their wings and buzz their way over desks and chairs stinging indiscriminately as they went. Bees cannot be confined to a classroom so, before long, they swarmed into the adjoining hall, distracting numerous children and not a few teachers! It was at this point that Mr Johnson decided to adopt the role of bee-keeper marshalling his charges and their lively queen bee back to their rightful hive.

Miss Fannakerpan remained undaunted. The following day, my art lesson was turned into a 'free-for-all' as small creatures became creative on windows, doors, floors and ceilings. Miss F. was demonstrating just how rewarding life could be when children were freed from inhibition. Whilst she gushed, I groaned. Whilst she enthused, I wilted. Whilst she gloried in successful enterprise, I wallowed in miserable failure. Who cleared the resultant mess? – NOT Miss Fannakerpan! When my Inspector suggested that the children should climb into school through the windows I felt that enough was definitely enough! My classroom windows were six feet above playground level, the elderly sash-type – likely to rival the guillotine in deadly potential. Should I risk the lives of youngsters in order to further my career? I refused Miss F.'s suggestion. Without a deal of enthusiasm, I was recommended as a fully qualified member of the teaching profession in the hope that I might, eventually, become more adventurous in my approach. After those traumatic experiences, I'm somewhat wary of experimentation. Thanks, Miss Fannakerpan!

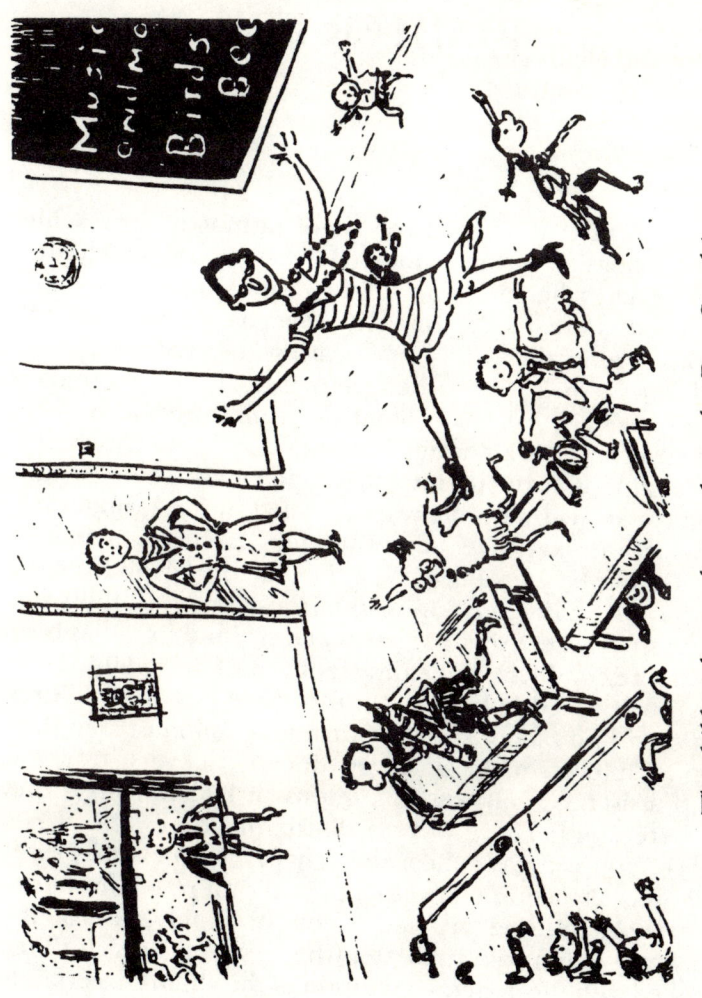

The children become bees – drawn by Ron Standring

CHAPTER FIVE

IN THE LATE 1940s, which saw the beginning of my teaching career, clogs were the school-day footwear of the children of Rochdale whereas, in my home town of nearby Bury, clog-shod feet were in the minority. Female Rochdalian mill-workers were still to be seen wearing the traditional clogs and shawls, their hair turned prematurely white by fluffs of cotton. It's a great shame that the young people of today will never see a living example of the 'lassie from Lancashire' made famous by the inimitable Gracie Fields. The only clogs to grace my feet were the wooden-soled variety brought into being by the exigencies of war and for which I was a 'guinea-pig' (father being manager of a shoe factory). Wooden-soled clogs were a poor relation of the iron-rimmed leathers that made sparks, kept the feet warm and dry and, so it has been said, were conducive to healthy foot growth in a child. These facts I attempted to bear in mind as three hundred children clattered into school each day drowning 'all music but their own'. Children of local clergy, doctors, lawyers, teachers, shop assistants, mill workers, guests of HM prisons – they all wore clogs. There was no discrimination of the classes where footwear was concerned. Thank goodness that every child was also equipped with a pair of pumps – plimsolls to those born outside my native county. If the state of the footwear didn't discriminate, the rest of the clothing, coupled with the general condition of the children, certainly did, though I hasten to add that by no means the larger percentage of working class children came under the heading of 'deprived' and or 'neglected'.

Joan was a tough nut. Nine years old, she was a latchkey child who bore the responsibility of six younger brothers and sisters. Whilst her mother regularly recovered from 'morning after the night before' symptoms, Joan would 'top and tail' the babies, dress the toddlers and prepare breakfast. At the end of each school day she would again be immersed in domestic duties. Little wonder that her academic progress left a lot to be desired. The poor child was too exhausted to concentrate her mind upon intellectual pursuits. One morning, when several degrees of frost had brought me to school wearing two of most things and three of some, I was disturbed to learn that Joan was huddled in a corner of the cloakroom. Our cloakrooms were places to be sought out when Lancashire temperatures soared to the eighties but to be careered through with speed during most of the year. A cloakroom in near-arctic conditions was certainly no place for the hardiest of hardy youngsters. Joan had coiled her lanky arms and legs around a solitary, tepid water pipe. Mr Johnson offered to look after my class during morning prayers leaving me praying that Joan would yield to my fervent entreaties before we both became victims of hypothermia. Eventually Joan and I began the thawing-out process in the luxuriant warmth of Mr Johnson's one-bar electric fire. My 'tough nut' was wracked by heart-rending sobs. Her normally pallid skin was now a blotchy crimson and the heat emanating from her pathetically thin body belied the sub-zero temperature. Joan wore a thin cotton dress topped by a threadbare cardigan. Not for her were woollen stockings and clogs but, instead, a toeless pair of dirty cotton ankle socks bursting out of a toeless, almost soleless, pair of filthy plimsolls. I succeeded in rubbing her hands until they were comfortably warm but she resisted all efforts to touch her feet. A male colleague came to my assistance. No matter how long I may live, the sight of those toes will live with me – hard, black, lifeless stubs – the result of severe frost-bite! Joan spent several weeks in hospital where expert attention saved the amputation of all but two of her toes. Her mother received a prison sentence for gross neglect and the children were dispersed among various foster parents.

David had been scavenging in dustbins and eating scraps of food intended for feathered friends of the area. Subsequent enquiries revealed that housekeeping money was employed in the backing of horses and the consumption of alcohol rather than the purchasing of food and clothing. Free school milk, free school dinners and a parcel of nutritious sandwiches, given to him at the close of each afternoon session, provided for David's inner needs whilst a fortuitous jumble sale catered for his sartorial requirements. The little lad was very proud of his two pairs of boots, nearly-new trousers, jacket, shirts and pullovers. Two days after the jumble sale, on a day of inclement weather, David presented himself, clad once more in the tattered rags of outgrown garments. The jumble sale acquisitions had been sold and the proceeds used to back the horse that took precedence over one small schoolboy.

Peter suffered from the complaint that even one's best friends are reticent to mention. He ponged something awful and no amount of fresh, industrial air could expunge the noxious odour. It was bad enough in the warmth of an Indian summer but, as autumn passed and winter developed so did Peter's pong. During PE and games lessons, the boys stripped to vest and shorts but, one day, when the ancient central heating system had run amok and temperatures were near tropical, I requested the removal of vests. 'Please Miss, mine won't come off,' said Peter. 'Stupid boy!' I thought, stalwartly ordering the child to draw nearer. Peter was right – his vest wouldn't come off! After a period of physical withdrawal (ostensibly to check some PE equipment but, actually, to fully inflate lungs) I made further investigation. The lad had been stitched into his underwear for the winter – a measure of misconceived bodily hygiene which assumed that the layer of warm air, trapped between body and underwear, must remain undisturbed until the return of balmy breezes. For enquiring minds, I convey the information that the underpants had vents at front and back but were firmly attached to the vest. Legs could be washed to a point above the knees and arms to just above the elbow. There was no excuse for dirt above shoulder level but the rest of the body would remain untouched for months. How I hoped for an early spring!

College training left me quite unprepared for the exercise of head-hunting and yet it was an art in which I was to become remarkably proficient. The school nurse still retains the title of 'nit-nurse' in the vocabulary of many present-day children on some of whose scalps nits are to be found happily nestling. *We* dealt with the fully fledged head louse and many were the fascinating periods I've spent watching several families of the species performing their athletic gyrations across an exercise book. Marking takes on an entirely new dimension when the red pen is required to adopt the sport of louse-dodging. My thick, shoulder length curls (self-made rather than God-given) were soon transformed into a shorter and more practical *coiffure* and, armed with tooth comb and special soap, I did frequent battle. The old head louse is no respecter of person! One particular variety had become efficient in dive-bombing tactics, using the wooden ceiling beams for take-off. Eyes in the top of the cranium would have been a useful addition in our classroom where we seemed to spend a deal of time with threats hanging, literally, over our heads. If variety be the spice of life, then we were well seasoned for the business of living.

Lice hunting – drawn by Ron Standring

CHAPTER SIX

You may be wondering how we staff members disported ourselves during our leisure time. I'm about to tell you. We taught from nine until twelve in the morning session and from two until four-thirty during the afternoon. Those of you who excel in the field of mental arithmetic will have realised, without recourse to calculators, that our 'dinner hour' was a misnomer – the 'hour' should have been in the plural! On every eighth day we were required to be on 'dinner duty' from noon until thirty minutes past that hour. Those of you adept in the art of short division will have realised that we were on 'dinner duty' every other week. To save further mental exertion, I'll tell you that we were 'free' for nineteen-and-a-half hours per fortnight and, as five of those hours were spent in food consumption, there remained fourteen-and-a-half to be filled with other activity. Forget not, dear reader, that all good teachers indulge in preparation of lessons; the construction of visual and/or auditory aids; the marking of books, etc., and must fit such indulgences into dinner hours, evenings or weekends.

We were a socially minded staff and those of us who remained sound in wind and limb fancied ourselves as sporty types. During autumn and winter months I joined young male colleagues in games of table tennis and, weather permitting, the months of spring and summer saw us disporting ourselves on the municipal tennis courts or, occasionally, managing a few holes on the municipal golf course. From time to time, the municipal swimming baths would be graced by our presence. At this point, I feel constrained to offer a vote of thanks to such a considerate municipality. Well done, Rochdale.

Mr Johnson knew somebody who knew somebody who was a committee member at Old Trafford so our staff sociability sometimes extended itself to Saturday cricket. There was a memorable occasion when, provided with packed lunches and teas, we settled ourselves to watch a test match. India, playing their second innings, were skittled out for little more than fifty runs leaving England victorious before we'd even thought about lunch. Pride in our team was clouded by the feeling that we hadn't really had our money's worth and to work this out we didn't need recourse to a calculator – a good thing, since they hadn't yet appeared on the market!

The stringent years of hostility extended into a lengthy post-war era and teachers of my generation still cringe when children are allowed to begin a new page of writing without using every available space on the previous page. We'd learnt how to manage with a minimum of necessities and to follow the adage 'Waste not, want not' to the letter. School outings were unknown in my experience but we were about to introduce them to our fourth year children. Today, school trips are exciting but part of the school curriculum – not so in my first teaching post! We waited impatiently for a local election to transform our school into a polling booth before arranging a 'get-away'.

Our first trip was ambitious – some used other words to describe the day trip to Warwick Castle! In these days of relative affluence when football fans book day-returns from Liverpool to West Ham without batting an eyelid, you may wonder why Rochdale to Warwick and back should have been considered ambitious. Bear in mind three things: less powerful engines, the absence of motorways and children with little, if any, experience of travelling even a *few* miles. We left school at some ridiculously early hour and had used our supply of Manchester Guardians (quality newsprint) before leaving that city behind us. Tissues and polythene bags were unknown quantities in 1949! The rest of the journey was completed with a lot of noise but without further untoward incident. Browsing through an old photograph album, I found a snap (a foreign word to todays children) in glorious black and white: a peahen and five chicks surrounded by a large group of young admirers from Lancashire. Other memories of what surely must have been a day full of incident escape me. Maybe the merciful shutters of memory have dropped or, perhaps, it was a day of pure enjoyment unsullied by disasters, natural or otherwise.

Our trip to York was marked by an unusual event. We'd done the customary tourist itinerary including scrambling up and down the hill to Clifford's Tower (several times!); walking a length of the wall; strolling along by the riverside; invading the Castle Museum and wandering, in a reasonably reverent manner, through the Minster. Now the time had come for each of the four groups to meet together for a restaurant tea. Three groups assembled but where was the fourth? After half an hour of waiting, the manager's restlessness and the rumbling of stomachs suggested that it would be expedient for three groups of children and three teachers to tackle their fish and chips, bread and butter, assorted 'fancies' and pots of tea. What could have happened to Alan and his dozen or so children? We phoned the police. A full scale search was underway. How glad we were that we'd reticently allowed some children to visit a fairground and that several of Alan's children were carrying prizes of goldfish in small glass bowls (plastic bags were not yet invented!). The police had 'something to go on' and, before very long, our missing children and their teacher were located at a police station seven miles distant from the centre of York.

Alan, a diabetic, had left home in a hurry forgetting his usual injection of insulin. Later in the day, amnesia overtook him. He remembered nothing between leaving the fairground and waking in a hospital bed. The children in his care had followed as he stumbled his way in the direction of Leeds. Eventually, he'd sunk to the ground in a coma and been found, surrounded by children, by a policeman who suspected him to be under the influence of alcohol.

On information from us, Alan was taken to the nearest hospital where he received the long overdue injection that restored him to consciousness. The recovered children rejoined the rest of the party and we travelled homewards, leaving Alan for a compulsory night in his hospital bed. Our story ended happily and no one was any the worse but, on future outings, everyone, staff included, wore an identity tag and carried a timetable of proposed venues. 'Better to be safe than sorry!'

CHAPTER SEVEN

For as long as I can remember, I've been a target for teasing and have thrived on it. The emergency-trained men singled me out as their butt for such practices and many were the occasions when resultant laughter vibrated through the school premises. Had I had any pretensions to self-importance, I would have been cut down to size pretty quickly. Young schoolmistresses of today, obsessed by the idea of equal status and women's lib, refuse to take the good-natured banter that puts things into a healthy perspective. I made numerous bloomers during my early years of teaching and they provided ammunition for my male colleagues who never missed a trick.

One day, I entered the staff-room to find Leslie and Jeff engaged in a rather puzzling escapade. This involved some sort of attempt to suspend themselves, horizontally, as near to the ceiling as possible. When I questioned their grotesque contortions, I was told that they were engaged in an important matter of research. Along with other spectators, I abandoned myself to a hilarious period of helpless laughter at the end of which I was led to my classroom and directed to the blackboard. The bold heading read 'Inverted Comas'. I, who prided myself on my spelling and considered myself a specialist in English language had, by omitting an 'm', changed the spoken word into a serious medical condition. The teasing rose to the surface at regular intervals and I was introduced to all and sundry as 'the girl who's safer on her full stops'.

On another occasion, I was approached by the same male

colleagues. They felt themselves under a moral obligation, being my senior in years and in wordly experience, to take me under their wings and give essential instruction in an area of my life where there had been gross neglect. To this end they had prepared suitable visual aids. Larger-than-life illustrations of bees and birds gave me a clue to the subject of their proposed lecture but I was 'in the dark' concerning my rather sudden need for such edification. A visit to my blackboard revealed, in my best blackboard writing the words: 'He lays his eggs in a nest made of grass and reeds and sits upon them until the baby birds crack their way out of the eggshell.' Are you surprised, that, to this day, I have a blackboard-complex and rarely leave writing on public view at the end of a lesson? 'Once bitten, twice shy.'

With that account of just two of my many gaffes, which continue to the time of writing, I leave behind the first five years of my experience in the noble profession of teaching. Recalling the period has brought a delightful sense of nostalgia but I am not deluded into thinking that all of my experiences were rosy. There were periods of gloom and despondency, coloured in varying shades of grey, but, invariably, the silver lining broke through to shatter doubt and disillusion. My farewell ceremony was a moving occasion both literally and figuratively speaking. The presentation gift was no surprise since I bought it myself with money donated, secretly, by children, staff, some parents and, I later learned, plain-clothes members of the local police. Children in my class were hopeless at the art of keeping a secret and, for weeks, had been thrusting sticky pennies, threepenny bits, and sixpences into *my* hands instead of handing them, surreptitiously, to one of the other teachers. Arguments raged as to who had made the greatest contribution and there were cries such as 'I brought sixpence,' 'I brought a penny seven times' and 'I brought a threepenny-bit twice and a penny two times – so there.' This last remark was accompanied by a hands-on-hip stance, a bending forward from the hips and a liberal protrusion of toffee-lined tongue. Though there was nothing wrong with my children's mathematical prowess, it is more than can be said for their grammar and humility. I would have told the biblical story of the widow's mite had I not been afraid that some of the more discerning donors might seek 'change' from their donations!

When all the money had been gathered, I was given the staggering sum of seven guineas (seven pounds and seven shillings) with which to purchase some article that I would enjoy and value. For months I'd looked longingly at a piece of jewellery set out in the middle of a window display of a select and expensive shop. Never before (and never since!) have I spent so extravagantly as on the day when I walked, as nonchalantly as I was able, into that jeweller's and bought that magnificent diamanté necklace. It was a treasure in its beauteous self and a treasure in the memories it evoked. It was worn on my wedding day, borrowed by our daughter for formal dinners at her university college and appeared when my husband and I gave a charity party in grateful celebration of our silver wedding. The necklace also lends credence to the proverb 'All that glistens is not gold.'

CHAPTER EIGHT

It was a foregone conclusion that teaching would finish once I achieved marital status. Not that married women were any longer debarred from teaching, as had been the case only a few years earlier, but because it was *infra dig.* to go out to work after marriage. Only the poorest of working class wives went out to work and, as the wife of a parson, I couldn't be considered as 'one of them' even though my husband probably earned less than did their working class husbands. Before our children were born, I answered one or two emergency calls from Lancashire Education Authority and 'filled in' at schools in the Colne area for brief periods but, as far as I was concerned, my teaching was finished. The subsequent arrival of two babies, separated by less than twelve months, provided a full-time job even without the distractions of a constantly burring telephone and door bells. My powers of oratory were now employed in addressing meetings and opening fêtes, garden parties and bazaars rather than imparting knowledge to junior minds.

Moving, after five and a half years, from the county of the red rose to that of the white, we settled down in a delightful part of the South Craven area of Yorkshire. As our lovely church, known locally as 'The Cathedral of Craven' despite it's noncomformity, celebrated its two hundred and fiftieth anniversary with events spanning the whole year, I became acquainted with more and more people. I suppose it was inevitable that one of these people just happened to be a head-teacher who just happened to be desperate for someone to teach her class of third year juniors for one day of each week, whilst she attended to administrative duties. The Headmistress in question was very persuasive, making me feel like an angel of mercy dropping manna from heaven! Our son had recently become a schoolboy and our four-year-old daughter was promised asylum, for one day each week, at the home of her best little friend. So it was that I began what was to be a three-year period at the adjoining village school. When the school roll rose above the two hundred mark, my workload doubled and transformed me into a two-day-per-weeker.

One particular event stands uppermost in my memory from this period. I was co-opted as assistant organiser of a 'mini Olympics' under the direction of the deputy head who was also the youth leader at 'our' church and a personal friend. If there is such a thing as a 'born' teacher, he was one of the finest. I became his willing assistant in this eminently educational venture. Competitors and erstwhile spectators familiarised themselves with the background of differing groups of participants from various countries of the world and found this to be a much pleasanter way of learning geography than memorising impersonal towns situated on impersonal rivers and serving impersonal ports. Art and craft came into their own as authentic looking flags rolled off the production line and medals of gold, silver and bronze came into being. Uniforms were designed for the athletic of all participating countries and seamstress-prodigies sewed deftly to individual measurements. Young carpenters fashioned a winners' podium with a modicum of skill and an excess of enthusiasm. Our project was under way with a vengeance – there was no stopping us now!

At last all was ready for the great day with athletes trained to a peak of perfection and the school playing field transformed into a stadium that would compete favourably with any previous Olympic rendezvous. My father, a temporary visitor, delightedly accepted the plum position of presenter-of-medals whilst my mother was all agog (as was her wont) at the thought of occupying a reserved seat in the VIP stand – staff-room chair on the front row! National flags fluttered

The Olympics – drawn by Ron Standring

bravely and attractively in warm sunshine and soft breezes. Young athletes disported themselves nobly; friends and relatives applauded rapturously; staff members organised frantically; father awarded magnificently and mother summed it up, succinctly, as 'a right rollicker!' She never spoke truer words!

My husband had been called to pasture new but, between resigning from my two-day-a-week post and actually leaving the area, came a request for a very short-term engagement at the school in which our two young children were being educated. The wily Headmaster waited until I'd agreed to help out before telling me that the class of which I was to take charge was that containing 'our two'. Karen was still of infant school age but had been promoted to join her brother (much to his disgust) in the first-year junior class. Whether this was because she was a young genius or because the infant department was over-subscribed escapes my memory, but the fact remains that mine was the prospect of tending my own lambs along with those of thirty or so other adoring mums! Karen and Michael were filled with elation, I with trepidation. Our normal happy relationship was on a two-to-two basis when Daddy was free and a one-to-two when he wasn't. It came as something of a shock to the children to find themselves sharing Mummy with thirty-six others and being firmly put in their place so that there could be no justifiable accusations of favouritism. As a mother they found me quite adequate – as a teacher, less than satisfactory! Within the home and family we continued to learn but I resolved never again to inflict myself upon our children in my professional capacity.

We were moving south to the Midlands which, according to a creditable English poet, are 'sodden and unkind'. The area around Nottingham with its Robin Hood associations sounded encouragingly exciting to all four of us but to our children in particular. For myself, I was extremely disappointed that the statue outside Nottingham Castle bore not the slightest resemblance to either Errol Flynn or Richard Greene!

CHAPTER NINE

ONE TREMBLES TO think what might have happened to the educational system of a certain area of the Midlands had not my husband tagged me along with him in the year of our Lord, nineteen hundred and sixty-five. Before the furniture had been put into position in our 'new' manse, a local Headmaster had phoned to stake his claim to my teaching services and, while our children were still discussing the merits and demerits of the two smallest among our five bedrooms, the local Area Education Officer had introduced himself by means of telegraph wire. We were in no doubt that God had called my husband to minister in this part of the country but it was very doubtful that I'd been called to rescue a collapsing educational structure! I wasn't born great; I have not, as yet, achieved greatness nor has anyone seen fit to thrust greatness upon me, so I must, reluctantly, assume that a dire shortage of teachers was the reason for my popularity. To cut a long story short, I was entreated, cajoled, persuaded into the service of Nottinghamshire Education Authority, though I succeeded in limiting my appointment to a temporary, part-time basis. Today, the position is completely reversed and it is the teacher who is entreating the authority!

Filling in the official application form was a mere formality although it gave me the opportunity to state age preference as juniors, seniors, infants – in that order. I was appointed to a local infant school! It didn't seem to matter that my last experience in such a school had been as a pupil, thirty-one years previously. What I didn't know about the teaching of infants was extensive, to say the least, but I was only going from nine until noon of each school-day. Imagine my shocked incredulity when I discovered that my afternoon counterpart had spent twenty years with senior girls as a home economics mistress! I definitely had the edge on *her* and my depressed confidence received a much needed boost. Fear not, ye parents of little ones, for such is the calibre of those of us who have the onerous honour of belonging to the once-noble profession that it matters not whether our pupil be six, sixteen or sixty. Our expertise includes adaptability and resourcefulness couched in all the modern jargon of our day – ongoing, in depth, at this point in time, a knock-on effect and the greatest of these is questionable!

Towards the end of my first term as part-time teacher in a temporary capacity, the sugared thumbscrews began to turn once more. 'We're absolutely desperate' was the first back-handed compliment. 'Could you come full-time for one term? Oh no, we won't insist on a permanent position. I really don't see how we can manage without you.' The flattery continued with such tongue-in-cheek phraseology as 'You've proved to be invaluable.' Insidiously, the honeyed words soften the will and, in simple, childlike trust, one signs yet another official form only to find oneself a permanent member of staff employed in a full-time capacity.

We had arrived in the Midlands just before Easter so it was on the first day of the summer term that Karen, Michael and I set out for school, each with a tummy full of butterflies. The children were bound for an elderly edifice of high, scholastic reputation. I was on course for the first built school on a relatively new campus. I knew very little about the reputation of 'my' infant school but had the distinct feeling that it was about to be lowered. Wishing to make a good impression on my debut, I arrived in good time and impressed the caretaker who informed me that it would be a good twenty minutes before other staff members put in an appearance. I was taken on a conducted tour by this cheerful and obliging young man and felt much less of a stranger knowing that I had found at least one friend. Then came the Headmistress – a buxom ('bonny', in Midland terms) woman in her late middle-age. Eyes piercing through thick double lenses seemed to give me far more than the customary once-over before she swept, like a ship in full sail, into her office beckoning me to join her. It worried her little that my experience in dealing with infants was nil and she despatched me, under escort, to view my classroom. The escort was not, as I supposed, the deputy head but the school secretary who filled me in authoritatively and with admirable aplomb. School secretaries are invaluable and, in knowledge of the fact, often exercise a 'greater than thou' attitude, putting teachers firmly in their place. Called to tasks beyond the demands of duty, they can be found ministering in the medical room, conveying casualties of playground or classroom to the nearest hospital, placating peevish parents or collecting cream cakes for end-of-term staff-room revels. Adaptability must be one of their foremost qualities and, if it can be allied to competency in typing, filing, repairing tape-recorders and decorating Christmas trees – then so much the better!

It was a surprise and a relief to discover that there were infant helpers available to assist in coping with buttons, shoelaces and natural accidents, thus allowing me to attempt the development of such skills as reading, writing, numberwork, art, craft and physical agilities – to mention but a few. The integrated day was in the process of development and I found it more than a little difficult to explain the intricacies of a certain number concept whilst Johnny banged a drum in one corner, Mandy offered cups of tea from the Wendy house and an enterprising group of potential Thespians acted out the story of Snow White and the seven dwarfs!

Our school was amongst those chosen for a pilot scheme to launch 'ita' – a system of teaching reading which, invariably, horrifies at first sight but which, put into correct practice, is amazingly successful. This experience brought me in on the ground floor in the basic skills of the teaching of reading. I never cease to marvel that most of us master the diversities of our English language and manage to read and write in a reasonably satisfactory manner. It's a skill taken very much for granted by those who possess it and causing tremendous frustration in the unfortunate who don't.

In a previous chapter, I stated that head-teachers come in various shapes and sizes and are of differing age and sex. The Headmistress of my first infant school was a rotund female approaching retirement and something of a Jekyll and Hyde character. Within school she was a veritable 'dragon' but people knowing her away from school premises described her as 'charming'. To children, teachers, ancillary staff, caretakers and parents she was a terror renowned for a facile ability to reduce even the stoutest character to a pulsating jelly. Tough members of the mining community would arrive at school heads high, shoulders back, chests fully expanded – very determined to put this mere female in her place. They left, drooping and dejected, pale shadows of their former selves. Small wonder that numerous people readily accepted the rumour that Miss Cookson had once taught in a borstal. I, for one, believe that teenage crime would have been considerably reduced had the rumour been fact!

Our head had trained to teach infants but confided to me that, whilst she could tolerate the seven-year-olds, she loathed the 'babies'. In her opinion, sniffing was a major crime and, since the majority of our children seemed untrained in the art of nose-blowing and rarely possessed material into which to blow, our school was largely populated by the criminal classes. Imagine the scene during morning assembly when, part way through 'All things bright and beautiful', an unsuspecting little child, situated on the front row, sniffed. The eyes behind the double lenses became furiously livid; nostrils dilated; two large, podgy hands grabbed the shoulders of the small child and proceeded to shake the tiny creature far more vigorously than you would shake a bottle of medicine before taking it. 'Why doesn't somebody stop her?' said I, after first witnessing such

The sniffing child – drawn by Ron Standring

a horrific spectacle. 'We're always too shocked to move,' was the reply and I came to learn the truth of what sounded, at the time, to be a feeble excuse.

Shall I ever forget the occasion when, with one hand, Miss Cookson carefully placed the figure of Mary into the nativity scene whilst the other hand was shaking the living daylights out of a small miscreant. What a travesty! Perhaps, as a pillar of the Anglican Church, this was her interpretation of 'Let not your right hand know what your left hand is doing'.

I had spent weeks and weeks patiently bringing a highly intelligent but extremely timorous little boy out of his shell and he was gaining in confidence day by day. No longer was it necessary for his mother to drag him to school. Brian knew that I would guard him from the Headmistress of whom he was so dreadfully afraid. There came a day when, with the best will in the world, I was unable to prise myself out of bed. I had become the victim of a virulent virus. After twenty-four hours of feeling intensely sorry for myself, thoughts turned to school and to Brian in particular. Two days later, I could contain myself no longer and dragged unwilling legs towards the educational edifice. Brian was not in school. Miss Cookson had chosen to victimise the smallest and most timid of my children and, in one day, had undone all my patient effort. Once again, Brian was disturbing the whole household with his screaming nightmares and was totally unfit, mentally and physically, to attend school.

It was no surprise when I recognised Brian's father approaching my classroom door the following morning but it *was* a surprise to learn that Miss Cookson couldn't see him as she was in charge of a class. There had been a full complement of staff during assembly! A spot of research revealed that Miss Cookson was indeed in an adjacent classroom so I went to inform her that Mr X. was waiting to speak to her. 'How can I see the man at this time in the morning when I'm in charge of these children – you'll have to deal with him.' It was seemingly irrelevant that I also was in charge of a class of children!

My way of dealing with Brian's father was to promise full

support when he complained to the education authority. Unfortunately, he preferred to accept the assurance that his son would be in no further danger from Miss C. Further research put me in possession of the fact that Miss Cookson, seeing Mr X. approaching the main entrance of the school had, with a remarkable turn of speed, burst into the nearest classroom. The surprised teacher had been ordered to go and do some checking of stock in the storeroom, a 'holy of holies' that we entered at our peril. Strange, under the circumstances, to remember how many times an infant helper had been left in charge of a class – why not on this occasion?

I am, generally speaking, of a placid nature but even the most placid among us can reach boiling point. I could not have been more livid! When playtime arrived, one assistant teacher went to 'play' with her Headmistress. There are times when loyalty to justice and fair play outweigh loyalty to authority. Miss Cookson was left in no doubt as to my opinion of her behaviour. She spent the next few weeks subjecting me to a crawling 'Uriah Heep' attitude – completely out of character for her and more than a little unnerving for me.

Our school had a cat and a rabbit, mainly because its Headmistress, who couldn't stand children, drooled over cats and rabbits – over one cat and one rabbit in particular. The cat was a bad-tempered creature and the rabbit was definitely unfriendly. I should know since, for some reason, I was in personal charge of feeding the cat and, with the help of my class, responsible for the well-being of the rabbit. I confess to being no lover of pet animals of any variety but very few people, staff or children, harboured affection for the two animals in question. The cat frequently bit the hand that fed it and the hand of anyone making a hand available! The rabbit lolloped into all manner of inaccessible places defying all efforts to return it to its restored-to-cleanliness hutch. Both creatures had free access to the staff-room where they were caressed fondly and addressed in crooning baby-talk by no less a personage than the headmistress herself. A scratch from the cat and droppings from the rabbit earned a loving 'Who's a naughty boy?' but a sniff from a child . . .! 'There's nowt so queer as folk!'

With the present surplus of teachers, it's difficult to remember that they were in short supply at the end of the 1960s. In our area, that shortage was most keenly felt in the infant schools. Our school was no exception to the general rule. In order to attract extra staff, a special responsibility post, carrying extra financial reward, was advertised. It was made quite clear that applications from existing staff would be a complete waste of time. An appointment was made. All that remained was for the Head and her Deputy to decide what the 'special responsibility' was to be. You'll never guess! The responsibility was that of caring for the school animals which could have been a veritable menagerie but, in fact, were one scruffy cat and a mangy rabbit. Maybe I should have kicked up a fuss and brought in the union – which would seem the popular thing to do in the present climate. I was profoundly relieved to relinquish what had been my unsought and unappreciated responsibility for far too long.

Whilst on the subject of special responsibility posts I mention just one, among many, farcical situations within my experience. I was delighted to hear that a former young colleague had received such a post. Her capability and conscientiousness made her fully deserving of such a position. When I rang to offer congratulations she said, 'You're not going to believe this. My special responsibility is looking after the school record-player!' Do you wonder at the title of this book?

The happy day came when Miss Cookson announced her impending retirement. She was about to tear herself away from the little creatures that she'd loathed for forty years. The Deputy Headmistress became responsible for planning the retirement ceremony and the collection for the inevitable presentation. One usually contributes towards a farewell gift in order to express appreciation of the beneficiary.

In this case, the contributions were expressions of profound relief and gladsome rejoicing.

Rumours began to circulate concerning Miss Cookson's successor. A teacher who'd been at the school before my arrival and who proved very unpopular was reported to have applied for the relatively lucrative position. Unhappy ex-colleagues remembered how Christine Clark had often boasted that she'd be the next head of our school. It seemed that no one had a good word for Christine. Learning that she was only twenty-seven years old and had been in no fewer than five schools during six years of teaching, I felt sure that those worrying about serving under her headship were wasting peace of mind. For one thing she was far too young to be given the responsibility of a large infant school. For another, her flitting from one school to another suggested an extreme instability. My confident predictions failed to convince the member of staff who requested immediate transfer. Who received the appointment? You're absolutely right – Christine Clark! Without going into details, I can report that this was yet another case of 'It's not *what* you know but *who* you know!' Christine was quite a good-looking lass and adept at turning on the charm.

CHAPTER TEN

IN MOST RESPECTS, our newly acquired Headmistress was as different from her predecessor as is chalk from cheese. (I can't help feeling that it's high time someone coined a phrase conveying a far stronger diversity – chalk and cheese can be identical in colour!) Christine was eminently eligible for membership of the Young Teachers' Society, Miss Cookson three decades past it. Christine was tall and slim, Miss Cookson short and dumpy. Christine had a 'with-it' hair style, liberally flecked with blonde streaks, Miss Cookson was a natural iron-grey with that 'had a bad night' look about it. Christine fluttered and spluttered in the presence of the opposite sex, Miss Cookson treated all males with a 'don't think you can pull the wool over *my* eyes' contempt – except when they displayed an appreciation of a certain cat and a particular rabbit whereupon she could become almost lukewarm toward them. Christine appeared to be fond of infant children (a point in her favour), Miss Cookson was positively aggressive in her attitude to them.

Some things they had in common. Neither of them was able to wear authority with the grace and humility that makes it beautifully efficient and eminently appealing. Both abused the power invested in them by members of the local education authority. Miss Cookson had a gross lack of control over her temper. Mrs Christine Clark had an inflated opinion of her own importance. Neither of them was able to relate to parents – in fact, both were positively rude in many instances. Does authority excuse one from the common courtesies of life? On the contrary! Both seemed to have the idea that the title of 'Headmistress' rendered them infallible and they were despots in their little realms. The door to my classroom was in the centre of the one, long corridor and become a 'Marjorie Proops Corner' where victims of dictatorial insensibility would seek a shoulder upon which to weep. More often than not, the weeping was literal and I was easily recognisable as the member of staff whose shoulder seams restricted full freedom of movement due to constant shrinkage!

For the first few days of Mrs Clark's rule, I enjoyed the moments when she flung open my classroom door with a cheery 'Good morning. Mrs Pilling – alright?' and I replied with an equally cheery, 'Yes, thank you, Mrs Clark.' After a week or so, the ritual was becoming somewhat hackneyed and I suspected that my superior was less interested in my well-being than she pretended and that my affirmative answer was often a white lie.

Mrs Clark held a staff meeting when she felt it necessary to inform us that *she* was the Headmistress and we would do whatever *she* said. Fighting talk – inclined to arouse a fighting spirit in her exclusively female audience. It seemed highly unlikely that psychology had been one of her strongest subjects during her college training!

Having been brought up in a Christian home, loyalty and respect for others had been fed to me along with my rusks and spinach! I was prepared to play ball and give to Caesar the things that belonged to him, but when 'our' Christine suggested that I was at fault in helping my seven-year-olds to read more fluently, to construct simple sentences, to spell common words and to develop an understanding of basic mathematics, then Caesar's authority just had to be questioned. 'They're only babies,' said my superior, 'let them play. They'll read when they're ready and, if they don't, they can watch TV. By the time they leave school, everyone will have calculators! You get too concerned about their progress. Relax and spend more time playing in the Wendy house.' Along with all the other activities involved in the teaching of older infants, I continued with the three Rs in spite of contrary orders from my superior.

The second major disagreement with 'Caesar' came when the latter decided that, during playtime, each classroom would be transformed into a tuck shop from which children could purchase such vitamin-packed foods as Jammy Dodgers, Fruity Chews and Iced Slices. It wasn't the twice daily transformation from teacher into shop-assistant and the consequent loss of tea-drinking leisure that was my chief complaint. Dentists of the British Isles were deploring the state of children's teeth and endeavouring to recruit parents, teachers, health visitors and others interested in child welfare in the battle against eating the wrong things at the wrong times. What sort of an example were we setting in even considering the introduction of 'tuck'? The mind boggled at the likely state of classroom furniture and floor when sticky fingers had made their imprint and small feet their implant! More serious still, the greater temptation to bully and/or steal likely to arise and the pressure on parents by children who felt they were missing out on a good thing. Our Headmistress was outraged when a number of us refused to become traders-in-tuck. This was mutiny! All manner of consequences were threatened but, knowing that the selling of refreshments was not a part of our contract, we remained unflinchingly adamant. The conflict was solved when two infant helpers set up stall at one end of the long corridor. Thieving and bullying increased and teeth rotted rapidly but school funds benefited so Mrs C. was happy!

Mrs Clark was the mother of a baby boy who must have had great difficulty in deciding which female to address as 'Ma-Ma-Ma-Ma' when the time came for him to produce meaningful sounds. For a period he was left with one or other of two near-neighbours until one moved away and the other took up full-time employment. When you're responsible for two to three hundred infant school children, you can't let your own child stand in your way so you shove him and carry-cot in the back of the car; stop off at your local hairdressing salon; dump son and impedimenta among wash-basins, perm solutions and hair-dryers and, promising to be back for your 4 p.m. appointment, leave the proprietress speechless as you accelerate away to fulfil your noble vocation. As if that isn't sufficient, you use the incident to entertain your staff, during morning break, expecting them to compliment you on your foresight and ingenuity. That contrary Mrs Pilling doesn't seem to be at all amused and, even when you mention that it is your intention to tip the hairstylist more generously than is usual, remains singularly unimpressed. That's the trouble with parsons' wives – strait-laced, narrow-minded and old-fashioned!

Imagine my thoughts when, one day, Mrs Clark said, 'I'm getting tired of mothers telling me that they've got a job. The minute their children are in school they're off to work. They can't wait, can they?' Do you, dear reader, have difficulty in deciding when is the time to speak and when the time to keep silence? Rightly or wrongly, I chose the former pointing out, in what I considered to be an infinitely polite manner, that the mothers in question waited until their children were at school before seeking employment. The point went home for Christine's instant come-back was, 'But *I'm* a Headmistress.' Why is it wrong for a shop assistant or a textile operative to leave a five-year-old but quite in order for a teacher to leave a babe-in-arms? It never ceased to amaze me that female teachers who have taken advantage of the short period of paid maternity leave can then stress the importance of the first five years of a child's life, criticising the mothers of the children they teach. Talk about removing 'the speck from your brother's eye' whilst ignoring 'the plank in your own!' In such a context the Bible seems very up to date. Teachers of above average intellect?!!

I had tolerated Miss Cookson in the knowledge that her retirement was imminent. Such was not the case with Mrs Clark, however. It was obvious to me that, for both our sakes, one of us had to go. I'd given three unwilling years to the teaching of infants (I'm grateful for such invaluable experience) so I made an appointment with the local Area Education Officer. He was full of concern for my future well-being and his fervent expression of thanks for services rendered reinforced the feeling that, had it not been for my arrival in the area, the whole educational system would have ground to a halt. He trusted that I was willing to continue in a permanent capacity. Actually, I'd been about to ask him about the possibility of a part-time appointment with juniors but he was such a charming man and I've always been a susceptible 'willing horse'. I left his office with the promise that I would be contacted well before commencement of the new school year and informed as to which local junior school I'd been appointed.

In spite of experiences that might have led to the contrary, I still have a deal of faith in my fellows, especially when they are in positions of authority and responsible for the well-being of others. Consequently, with little more than a week of the summer term remaining, I refused to phone 'them' feeling sure that 'they'd' contact me as promised. My faith was justified! Once again the Authority was at its wit's end! No one could be found to fill a post in a school some miles away from home – certainly beyond my walking or cycling distance. I was pretty athletic for my age but by no means a superstar. 'Is the position with juniors?' was my first question. 'The school is mixed infants and junior girls,' came the reply. 'Is my appointment with junior girls?' I asked, becoming somewhat suspicious. 'It's a very important class. Transitional between infants and juniors.' My suspicions deepened. 'The Headmistress is desperate.' My life was fast becoming strewn with head-teachers in various stages of desperation. I maintained silence, determined to play this one cool. 'She's a lovely person and wants someone experienced and efficient.' Are you getting the feeling that you've heard this sort of thing before?

To cut a long story short, I agreed to accept a one-term appointment at Kimberwood Junior Girls and Mixed Infants. About to begin was another chapter in the book of my teaching life. By this time in my varied career, I had reached that magical age at which life begins and, after which, one used to require fortifying! Young people of the last decade or so have become so delicate that the fortifying is now necessary during their late twenties. Perhaps it's less a deficiency in the young and more a lack of demand for a certain commodity bearing a well-known trade name.

CHAPTER ELEVEN

IN AGE AND inconvenience, Kimberwood Junior Girls and Mixed Infants was rather similar to my very first teaching academy. Classroom windows afforded a rather restricted view of the sky and allowed access to the sort of air whose freshness was open to debate. The drone of traffic was a constant background to all educational activity. Lofty brick walls enclosed the stone-flagged playground which was bordered, along one side, by outside toilets. One redeeming feature, not present in many modern playground areas (future planners please note!), was a shelter to which children and the teacher on duty could repair when falling rain or biting wind made the great outdoors less than comfortable. Sometimes to be seen from the playground was a funeral cortège winding its way slowly up the steeply ascending slope of a nearby hill at the top of which stood the local cemetery-church. Is it irreverent to suppose that the original planners of this particular cemetery were intent on giving their clients a lift upon their way?

Physical details of the school and its environs were noted during my preliminary visit. A member of Kimberwood staff met me at a pre-arranged rendezvous and I was on my way to make the acquaintance of yet another Headmistress. During the past three years, my natural optimism had been fighting a losing battle and my inculcated respect for teachers in general, and heads in particular, had become seriously jaundiced. The ensuing months were to effect a radical change in the situation.

The Head's room at Kimberwood was reminiscent of that

of my Rochdale school. At my moment of entry it was providing a refuge and eating-place for those members of staff not employed on dinner-duty. Their relaxed attitude spoke well for the buxom little woman who stepped forward to greet me. A warm, firm handshake, a face creased with laughter wrinkles and eyes twinkling with good humour. Instant rapport was established. From that moment, my waning confidence in the teaching profession began its recovery. For the first time, in what seemed a very long period, I felt I could hold my head high and take pride in being a teacher.

Miss Kay had the love and respect of teaching staff, pupils, ancillary staff, parents and the old people of the neighbourhood who were regularly invited into school to meet the children, enjoy a cup of tea and be encouraged to feel a real part of our happy family. The atmosphere was pervaded by Christian love, actively displayed in genuine sharing and caring. There was nothing sloppy or sentimental about it – simply a recognition of Christianity as a way of life, not just something initialled R.E. on the timetable. The majority of the children, most of whom came from a salt-of-the-earth working class background, were courteous and cooperative in a natural and friendly manner. There was none of your cringing subservience and certainly none of the brash impudence, even obscene vulgarity, evidencing itself within certain schools at the present time. Naughty children were regarded, by peers and teachers alike, as letting down the family and were usually brought back into line before reaching the problem stage. Miss Kay exerted a firm but kindly discipline and, whilst not suffering fools too gladly, was at least prepared to offer them the benefit of the doubt.

In common with many members of my profession, I've always encouraged the use of litter baskets. Children have never left my room, at the end of the school day, without first inspecting the floor area beneath their desk or table and removing anything despoiling the surface thereof. Maybe we've intruded upon the preserves of that noble army of school cleaners but have not, as yet, been confronted by any of their shop stewards. Whilst my classrooms have been havens of ultimate tidiness, such can certainly not be said for the playgrounds of schools in which I have taught. Outdoor litter bins mean different things to different children. They can be one strut of a goalpost, a cricket wicket, a base for ticky, or a thing to be jumped over (or, by the less athletic and the unobservant, tripped over). Only a very small percentage of children recognise a litter bin as a receptacle for waste of description various.

For how long are heads going to face school assemblies and put the question: 'Where must you put your litter?' For how long are they going to suffer the parrot-like response: 'In the litter bin.' For how long are they prepared to gaze upon playgrounds ankle-deep in sweet wrappers, crisp bags, banana skins and orange peel, periodically (especially when governors are due to inspect) sending posses of litter-pickers. How to solve this problem has exercised many superior minds. Miss Kay found a very successful answer.

Donning my coat, before embarking on my very first spell of playground duty at Kimberwood, I was almost bowled over by an agitated infant. What dire tragedy had befallen during my brief absence from the scene of battle? The shocked horror on the face of the child confronting me suggested an event of catastrophic proportion. My vivid imagination (sometimes a blessing, sometimes a positive menace) had me pleading extenuating circumstances in a Court of Law (but I was already asking myself if the donning of outdoor apparel was sufficiently extenuating). Stiff upper lip; superb control; outward calm; inner turmoil: 'What's the matter dear?' 'Nigel's eating a tuffy' (toffee). 'But that's alright dear – it's playtime.' 'T'int' (it is not). 'We can't 'av tuffies at school.' Further investigation revealed that this child of such tender years spoke the truth, the whole truth, and nothing but the truth. I must point out that Nigel was a newcomer to the school and, therefore, an innocent offender.

Miss Kay had been among those innumerable heads oft posing the question: 'Where do we put our litter?' and receiving the oft-repeated response: 'In the litter bins.'

Child's conception of a litter-bin – drawn by Ron Standring

Deciding that the response was purely theoretical, she had issued an ultimatum: 'You have a choice. Either you bring sweets to school for playtime consumption and put the wrappings in the litter boxes or you do not bring sweets to school at all.' For a day or so, the litter bins fulfilled their intended function but then children became forgetful. Once more the ground took precedence and the playground reverted to its litter-strewn state. There were no further warnings. From that day, not a child brought a single sweet to school apart from the unsuspecting Nigel who was speedily brought into line by the converted. Not one parent became militant concerning the rights of his, or her, child, or children. Not one advisor raised his, or her, hands in horror at this outrageous interference with the child's right to exercise his, or her, free will. Not one member of staff was heard to express the feeling that, on this occasion, 'The Boss' was going just that bit too far. Come to think of it, Kimberwood is the only school, in my teaching experience, in which the head-teacher was never referred to as 'The Boss'. Such a designation was unnecessary. Just and respected authority was of the calibre that required no elucidation and explains, in the proverbial nutshell, the total acceptance of an extreme decision. Miss Kay never pretended to be perfect. Those displaying the greatest pretensions to perfection are usually those the farthest from it. Our Headmistress had the relatively rare gift of being able to laugh *at* herself but laugh *with* others.

A few weeks before the end of my first term at Kimberwood I was asked, by the Headmaster of a junior school in my home town, to take up a position in his school. I knew the school well. Our children had benefited greatly from their few years of education within its walls. It was a *junior* school! The temptation was great but Miss Kay deserved consultation before I made up my mind. She and her staff had accepted me as one of the family and one doesn't leave family lightly. I was humbled when my Headmistress begged me to complete the school year and help her to enjoy her retirement celebrations. She'd won the day even before promising that I'd be in receipt of a splendid testimonial and would be appointed to a suitable junior school even if she had to twist the arm of the Area Education Officer.

The whole of that year at Kimberwood was exhilarating but the last few weeks made a particularly strong impression. Miss Kay was retiring after forty years of teaching, the final fifteen of which had been spent as Head at Kimberwood. Her Deputy, Miss Black, was also retiring. Miss Black had spent the whole of her teaching career at Kimberwood and had taught three generations of children. Grandparents, coming to admire their grandchildren's prowess in school concerts, reminisced about their experiences in Miss Black's class. If they were to be believed, and there seems little reason to doubt their veracity, Miss Black had come in like a lioness and was going out like a lamb. I was going out with them after a mere three terms of service at Kimberwood. They had given respective lifetimes of service to the teaching profession whereas I had yet to reach the half-way mark. Nautically speaking, they were 'tying-up' for good whilst I was merely 'changing boats'.

On the Saturday preceding the final day of Misses Kay and Black's professional career, teaching staff and ancillary staff of Kimberwood School were their guests on a memorable outing. A 'slap-up' meal at an eminent restaurant was followed by attendance at an open-air performance of a Gilbert and Sullivan operetta in the grounds of Newark Castle. This typically generous gesture was enjoyed and appreciated by hostesses and guests alike, a happy family occasion to be cherished among the souvenirs of memory.

The retirement party and presentation amounted to far more than the formal, traditional affair. There was no need for the bottled spirit as more than enough of the genuine variety emanated from the hearts of those present and the greetings of those absent. Official words, from the Area Education Officer, were markedly sincere leaving no doubt as to the degree of gratitude felt toward good and faithful servants who had run an admirable race.

Miss Kay had fulfilled her earlier promise and I had been

appointed to the junior school on the same school campus as my previous infant school. Thanks, Miss Kay, for restoring me to juniors and, even more important, for restoring my creaking confidence in the noble profession of teaching.

CHAPTER TWELVE

THE SCHOOL CAMPUS of which I speak was in 1969, and remains in 1992, an impressive place comprising four school buildings separated by playing fields and landscaped areas. Thirteen years ago the schools were designated as infant, junior, secondary modern and technical-grammar. All the schools are named in memory of a female county councillor who had a great concern for the adequate education of the children of this area. For the purpose of this book she will be known as Alice Holdoor or A.H. for short.

I was joining the junior school not as a replacement but as an additional member of staff – one trained in teaching of ita. Already one staff member was expert in the art but the numbers of children coming from the infant school and not yet transferred to traditional reading was far more than could be contained in one class. Being predominantly concerned with teaching seven-year-olds to read and write seemed a long way removed from the physical education and geography lessons for senior children that had occupied a good deal of my time during teacher training but at least I was out of an infant school. Why was I so delighted to be back in a junior school? Because I was a member of a mixed staff. There were men among my colleagues! No longer would staff-room conversation centre around Mrs So and So's latest operation or the juiciest bit of scandal gleaned whilst under the drier. There was now the strong possibility of such topics as cricket, football, athletics, economics and politics being among the content of conversation and I still harboured hopes of good-natured ribbing and humorous banter becoming the order of the staff-room. As yet I was known only as the parson's wife and it was several weeks before I was told that I'd been regarded as a potential dampening restriction on future staff-room activities. There are definite disadvantages to marrying a parson!

I had met the Headmistress before on those occasions when she had visited my classroom in the infants section of the campus in order to get to know those children shortly to be transferred to the juniors. I'd been favourably impressed and looked forward to developing our brief acquaintanceship. It wasn't long before we discovered that we were both Lancastrians and that whilst her daddy had taken her as a little girl to watch Preston North End my daddy had taken me to watch Bury – 'The Shakers'. She had abundant knowledge of the intricacies of the game of football and was frequently to be found among the men discussing the finer points of the latest League or Cup game. Miss Starbrick had a very good knowledge of and relationship with the children and a remarkable ability for remembering their names, even years after they'd left our school. Her sleuthing, not requisite of the job but an invaluable commodity, rivalled that of Sherlock Holmes. When invited to a Buckingham Palace garden party our Headmistress brought her ensemble to school and gave us a 'twirl' in the staff-room. We were proud of her appearance and proud of the leadership qualities that lay behind the invitation and which reflected strongly upon the school. I wasn't surprised to learn that Miss Starbrick had already attended a royal garden party several years previously when she'd already given years of service to the school.

On my arrival, the school, built to accommodate three hundred and sixty pupils, had five hundred on roll and two dining halls were in use as classrooms. During the first few years of what was to be my fourteen-year session at A.H. Juniors, two cloakrooms and one drying-room were converted and the dining-rooms reverted to their original use. Later, when I became a special needs teacher, the drying-room was mine until I was promoted to one of the excloakrooms. This proved admirable when the long, heavy curtains from our very first manse ('Don't throw them away, they might "come in" ') were eventually replaced by a draught-excluding attractive brick wall which had the added advantage of promoting privacy. That ex-cloakroom was mine until teaching days were done and, despite occupational hazards, its memories are predominantly happy ones.

We served a large council estate, a smaller council estate and an area of privately owned property – that was our catchment area. As with the majority of state schools our children including some deprived, neglected, and abused, a number who were over-cared for and cossetted, and a very good number of average, normal, healthy, well-cared for children. Lest, in this class-ridden society, you assume a wrong impression let me say that the three types of children were spread across the private and council sectors. We had more than our fair share of disruptive children but, as in my first school, they were, with the very occasional exception, good-hearted, willing and happy and amenable to firm and kindly discipline. You may have noticed that such discipline is high in my priorities. I commend it to students and young teachers. Firmness alone can become despotic. Kindness alone can become slackly sloppy. The two together can build and achieve, encourage and inspire.

Structurally, the school was – and still is – impressive. Eighteen years old when I first entered its portals, it was by far the most modern school in which I'd ever taught. I was struck by the vast amount of natural light streaming through generous windows allowing vistas of trees, shrubbery, grass, flowers, sky, racing clouds – all those appealing sights that were shut out by nineteenth and early twentieth century architects as deterrents to concentration. I discovered that my classroom windows, like those of the other rooms, apart from converted drying-room and cloakrooms of future days, included French windows. On balmy days when the aforementioned French windows were not rendered inoperative due to subsidence, the scourge of most buildings in a coalmining town, we could throw them open, walk through them on to a terraced area and, thence, onto wide open lawns. Suitable lessons could be taken in pleasant surroundings whilst fresh air and shafts of soothing sunlight caressed pupils and teacher alike. Less than half a mile away heavy traffic roared past on a busy road but no sight or sound of it disturbed us. Other windows were numerous and opened freely letting in all the East Midland breezes required to freshen one teacher and thirty-nine first-year juniors. Having mentioned the advantages of maximum window space it seems only fair to point out that they tended to make the classrooms akin to ice houses in winter and hothouses in summer. As they say 'You can't have it all ways!'

Writing about A.H. Junior School has given me a good excuse for looking through annual staff photographs. There are well-known familiar faces that appear year after year and others that appear but once or twice whose faces stir the chords of memory but whose names are lost in oblivion. When I joined the staff in 1969 we were sixteen strong, excluding Miss Starbrick. During the following fourteen years our numbers varied between that number and twenty-three. One or two classroom-helpers were appointed and a deaf unit and special needs unit led to increased staffing.

During my first year of teaching children not yet transferred from ita, I was fully occupied and, although other subjects required by the curriculum were not neglected, reading was my priority. Fortunately the children were as keen as I and gradually, then with growing momentum, transference occurred until, with just about three weeks of the summer term remaining all 'my' children were on t.o. and reading 'proper'. At the beginning of the next school year, an edict came from County Hall that no teacher was to have more than forty children on register. The number of itas from the Infants had increased so I had thirty-nine on my register and a further three joined us each day from a neighbouring class. That way we managed to remain within the law and still gave the necessary help to all children awaiting transference to t.o.

This was to be the last year that we would be dealing with

ita as the Infant School had dropped it altogether. Many of us, having experienced the great advantages of the scheme, felt this to be a retrograde step but recognised the difficulty facing children – moving from an ita school to a t.o. school and vice versa – and parents frustrated at being unable to help their children with this new fangled alphabet. Isaac Pitman of shorthand fame devised ita so it's nothing new! Oldham is the town which experimented first and, after fantastic results, recommended it to the rest of the educational world. Publishers now ceased to present children's readers in ita so it died a regrettable but necessary death.

Before leaving the subject of ita, upon which I could wax more lyrical than I already have, let me tell you of a young student-teacher who worked with me during early 1971. Talking with her on her preliminary visit I discovered that she'd recently gained an honours degree in classics. I tried to prepare her for the cultural shock that would hit her when she met my children. How wrong can one be? She took to the children and they to her. When she left us after that first day she took with her ita teachers manuals and came back fully prepared in theory and suitably enthused. For the four weeks of her teaching practice she taught ita with small groups within my class and, at the close, was as much in love with it as she was with her classical languages. She didn't want to leave and I didn't want her to go.

I never met a teacher whose initial reaction was other than adverse. I commented that I was grateful that our two children hadn't been faced with that stupid language whilst others summed it up in one word, usually 'crazy' 'mad' or 'ridiculous'. I never met a teacher who, after a few weeks of teaching this alphabet, wasn't full of praise for it and thoroughly enthused by it. Most, if not all, reading schemes will work if properly taught by keen and eager teachers. The same applies to every subject providing the children are also enthused. Having written those words, I wonder where my science teachers slipped up! They seemed enthusiastic for their subject but never managed to enthuse me! I'm grateful that an ita pilot scheme was in operation when I was thrust into teaching infants because it brought me in on the ground floor giving me the opportunity to open the wonderful world of reading to many children. Reading means, and has meant, so much to me over so long a period that I can't bear to think of anyone deprived of the art.

CHAPTER THIRTEEN

PART-WAY THROUGH the autumn term our Senior Master casually remarked, on entering the staff-room during morning break, that he'd knocked up a script for a staff pantomime. Knowing him to be a keen and quite brilliant amateur actor and to have an inventive and witty mind we took him very seriously but were somewhat perturbed to find that he'd involved all the staff with the sole exception of Miss Starbrick. How could we leave our Headmistress, on the last school-day before Christmas, to shepherd five hundred and fifty excited children into the Hall single-handed? Not that she couldn't, or wouldn't, do it but it was unfair to expect it of her. It was surprising how many of us volunteered to forego our roles in the name of duty and deference to our Head! What a thoughtful and considerate group of teachers. Eventually, one female teacher known by herself and recognised by the rest to be entirely incapable of cavorting on stage, or anywhere else for that matter, was selected as Headmistress's helper with assistance from one male whose presence on stage, in everyday dress, was required only toward the close of the production.

Through all the kerfuffle of the playtime break I'd learnt that this staff pantomime was a first-time enterprise. I assumed that rehearsals would take place during dinner hours which were, in those days, nearly two hours long. Nothing of the kind! This was obviously to be a mammoth undertaking with rehearsals, an hour at the minimum, after school twice a week to begin with and more often if necessary. To preserve utter secrecy, all children were to be well away from the premises before the cast assembled on or around stage. We were indeed fortunate in our stage facilities, so much so that local dramatic societies frequently hired the hall to present their current productions.

Some of the rehearsals conflicted with prior engagements, ranging from getting to the local shop before closing time to dealing with other pressing matters. Until the final ten days of term arrived, I can't remember a single rehearsal during which our Senior Master and producer wasn't standing-in for missing characters. We forgot our words, we gave wrong cues and we made our entrances from the wrong side. We were worse than juniors but we got great fun out of our thespian activities and a closer relationship with one another.

Our first pantomime was called 'The Missing Lost Property Box' since that article was constantly mentioned in classrooms and in Assemblies. When children lost something, as some did with monotonous regularity, it was 'Go and look in the lost property box.' When they found something, which some did with equally monotonous regularity, the refrain was similar: 'Go and put it in the lost property box.' So that the children might harass their long-suffering teachers less often we would have a rehearsal at the end of an assembly when in answer to Miss Starbrick's question 'Where do we put lost property?' five hundred children would chorus 'In the lost property box, Miss Starbrick.' This was followed by: 'What do we do with property we have found?' 'Put it in the lost property box, Miss Starbrick!' So you will understand that the lost property box loomed large in our minds. Our pantomime had the elements of mystery and suspense besides the fun and jollity of Tweedle-Dum and Tweedle-Dee, Simple Simon and many other favourite pantomime characters.

I had been given the part of The Good Fairy – typecasting according to colleagues – and I took that as a compliment whether or not it was true. Having nothing in my wardrobe remotely resembling the garb of a fairy, finding nothing useful in our daughter's wardrobe and not even looking in

The author as the Good Fairy
drawn by Clare & Rachel Pilling

our son's, I found myself where I had often been and have since been again – in a quandary. Having, to date, given you a picture of near perfection, I now shatter what was a misconception anyway and confess that I am hopeless with a needle, apart from sewing on missing buttons and darning socks when absolutely necessary. To create the dress of the fairy that would enchant five hundred and fifty children, give or take a few hardened eleven-year-old boys, was beyond my ken. Appealing to our art specialist, herself a gifted actress and stylist, brought its reward and she furnished me with a pale pink froth of a dress. Teamed with a tinsel tiara and a suitably trimmed broom handle, I was transformed and translated. How proud and happy was I to restore, by a final wave of my wand, the missing lost property box with the fervent approval of the packed-to-capacity audience. Who says nobody loves a fairy when she's forty? I was forty-two!

Our pantomime really was a resounding success and worth all the time and effort expended. As Christmas of each succeeding year approached we would hear first-year children being told that the teachers would be doing their pantomime on the day before the holiday started. For five or six years this proved to be the case. Imagine how old the Good Fairy was becoming, nearer fifty than forty! At the time of writing I have reached the stage at which one has difficulty in remembering some of the finer details and, apart from Batman and Robin and one in which Long John Silver talked very successfully with the parrot perched on his shoulder, my mind is a blank. 'Why did the Pantomimes come to an end?' you might ask. 'I'm not sure', I might answer. Maybe the inventive genius of our Senior Master ran dry. Perhaps my pink dress was bursting at the seams – it certainly looked the worse for wear. Could it have been the advent of a new Head? I suspect it was a mixture of all three. I wonder if any of the thousand children who came under the spell of our performances ever tell their children at Christmas time of the remarkable talent of those who taught them. Do they perhaps say, as one is wont to do,

'They don't make 'em like that today!' Readers may feel that it's not a bad thing!

If treading the boards was our winter activity, as a relief from teaching (and not as a substitute for it), so activities on the playing field became our recreation during spring and summer terms. I had volunteered as goalkeeper in the staff versus school First Eleven Match. What junior forward would hurl himself, or ball, against the inoffensive Mrs Pilling, I thought, I'm onto a cushy number. Miss Starbrick, who had watched our school team at every opportunity and knew the members well, assured me that the lads would be unsparing and their strikers could kick a ball with some force. I bowed to her superior wisdom and became right back. Only a few minutes into the game I was struck in the face by a galvanising shot that rose from the boot of a four-foot cherub. With a head that seemed to have increased drastically in girth and had pretty stars bursting around it I clung to my nearest team-mate who happened to be a handsome young student. I must admit that I thoroughly enjoyed that part of the game. I can't remember volunteering for more football and think that Miss Starbrick must have been afraid of losing staff involved in activities beyond the realms of duty.

Rounders was the next sport to be indulged in. The staff team went up on the notice board and although pleased and proud to be listed, I had other plans and, therefore, presented my profound excuses. On the day of the game, sunny and warm, I changed into trainer's strip and ran to the pitch at half-time festooned with towels and carrying a bucket of icy cold water and my husband's outsize car-cleaning sponge. Most of the staff team were grateful to have a spongeful of icy water squeezed over their heads and down the back of their necks. It was obvious that the spectators were enjoying the spectacle from the roars of approval so I exaggerated my actions more than ever, allowing water to flow from ever increasing height. It was unfortunate that the Senior Mistress had had an expensive perm the previous evening. She was not amused. Well, you can't please all of the people all of the time!

Netball and the noble game of cricket came within our orbit as sporting teachers but our knowledge of the rules left a lot to be desired. What could be more ignoble, as was my lot, than to slink from the field of play having committed a foul upon a child to whose all-round education you've pledged yourself wholly and inextricably. One has to trust that the shutters of memory will be kind.

Miss Starbrick was a good sport in allowing such competitions between staff and children. We weren't in competition to illustrate our superior prowess. On more than one occasion 'the boot was on the other foot'. I think that we wanted the children to see us as fellow human beings and surely that could only have been good.

There is a purpose to the title of this book. I could have taken you painstakingly through the diverse elements of a junior school curriculum. Would you have enjoyed reading such a book? I certainly wouldn't have relished writing it!

CHAPTER FOURTEEN

Do you recall my comments about the sparsity of school trips during my first five years of teaching? During my final years of teaching, a class of children would feel itself very shabbily treated had there been fewer trips than two in a school year. One trip might have been to a museum or exhibition displaying articles related to some classroom topic. Such trips were usually to places in relatively close proximity to school. The second, and probably the most favoured, would be to a theme park, a safari park or perhaps even to the seaside, which is so far removed from the North Midlands. Excitement was always at a premium and, for weeks before, children could be overheard saying 'I can't wait . . .'.

During my final eleven years of teaching, I was not a class teacher, drawing instead small groups of 'ESN' (educationally subnormal) children, grouped as special needs today – from the six or seven classes of the Lower Junior School. However, I was not overlooked when trips were being organised. I was allocated to a particular class to help its teacher and those parents nobly volunteering their assistance. I must be one among many teachers who have found a school trip to be even more stressful and exhausting than a day of concentrated teaching. Happily, whilst I trust I shared the load, I was spared the full burden of responsibility and remember many of those trips with equanimity. Twycross Zoo still conjures up the sight of animals who looked contented in their well-kept enclosures and accepted their food from attendants who seemed concerned for their highest welfare. Drayton Manor Park provided an enjoyable outing and the enjoyment of swings, slides and rides was evidently worth the rather excessive queuing time. Markeaton Park suggests blue skies, fluffy white clouds, acres of open grassland and, eminently suitable for a day of almost tropical heat, freely accessible, shallow paddling pools for falling into accidentally or on purpose.

Perhaps Gunthorpe Bridge brings back the very happiest memories. I was with one of my favourite male colleagues and his class of thirty-eight nine-to-ten-year-old children. The day was balmy, neither too hot nor too cold.

We walked the length of the locks and past the weir with something new to see and interesting to watch the whole of the way. Our picnic was eaten on the grassy bank by the bridge. Rather than have individuals on sorties to the toilets, we gathered them into orderly lines of eighteen boys and twenty girls. I knew where to go with the girls, I'd been to Gunthorpe Bridge before! As we queued in a corridor, more than one child whispered 'Isn't it nice, Mrs. Pilling?' It was and it wasn't until we'd finished our ball games and were on our way to rejoin the coach that I realised that we ladies had patronised the Gunthorpe Bridge Hotel! No wonder the decor had been vastly superior to that of the average public toilet! I was always the sort of teacher keen to give children of the very best.

I come now to the trip that has etched itself most firmly into my mind and became the one never to be forgotten. Mr Unloss, my equivalent in the Upper Juniors, asked me to accompany him and twenty-four of his 'special' children on a day in London. Mr Unloss had taken admirable safety precautions prior to the trip and, on the day in question, we each sported a jumbo-badge bearing upon it the name of the school, the individual, the two teachers in charge, London venues to be visited and times of such visitations. A local bus took us to Nottingham railway station.

The station platform was packed to suffocation with children and teachers. Fortunately the special train on which we were to make our epic journey was divided into labelled compartments and, even more fortunate, Alice Holdoor Juniors had a compartment all to ourselves. Few of our children had ever been on a train before and excitement was at fever pitch. There is no doubt that the toilet was the biggest attraction and it was occupied during every mile of our not inconsiderable journey. The girls, perhaps with an inborn recognition of there being safety in numbers, occupied it in parties of two or three at a time.

We arrived at St Pancras and began our frantic attempts to separate our children from other school parties as we headed for the Underground. Although we'd done our best to prepare the children for confrontation with a 'tube' train, screams of terror predominated as the clashing, metallic monster materialised out of the black tunnel. Automatic doors with their pincer-like movement froze some of our charges but, eventually, with me pulling and Mr Unloss pushing, we crammed them all in. What a cultural shock we must have been for those poker-faced Londoners on their way to a day at the office or the shop or elsewhere. With each jerk of the coach the children flung themselves upon people's knees, hung onto their coats or stood upon their feet whilst giving free rein to their East Midland accents with strident voices. All sharing our coach knew their teachers' names because, though separated by twenty yards in some cases, they courteously included us in conversation. Mr Unloss was invariably aspirated becoming Mr Hunloss whilst I, losing my last letter, became Mrs Pillin'.

Keeping well within our timetable we boarded the boat that would take us to the Tower. As a tidily uniformed little girl made to pass us, one of our girls stuck out a leg and tripped her. I'd seen it all so clearly and knowing it to have been no accident my hand made an immediate impression upon the fleshy portion of the offender's leg. A short sharp blow strategically placed saves any amount of futile nagging. The child who had been sent sprawling across the boat deck had suffered because she was 'posh' and, aware that the assailant wore second-hand clothes which were often dirty and torn, a part of my sympathy was with her.

All I remember from the visit to the Tower is persuading a group of the boys away from a crafty game of raven baiting to prevent them from being accosted by a Beefeater. Crown jewels to see, instruments of torture to behold, chain-mail at which to marvel but raven persecution preferable.

Westminster Abbey was our next highspot so we wended our way through busy London streets. Street stalls grabbed the attention of our children whose liberal supply of spending money had been burning holes in their pockets ever since we left Nottingham. We were surprised at the amount of money they'd been given especially as the majority were on 'free dinners'. Most children were persuaded of the wisdom of postponing their buying until later thus avoiding carrying merchandise, beside packed lunches, around the metropolis. Even so the stalls attracted the children. We employed frequent roll-calls feeling it to be better to be safe than sorry. As we were about to enter the ancient and majestic portals of the Abbey I had a distinct feeling that our number had dwindled. A quick but thorough count registered only nineteen. We'd counted just before crossing the difficult width of thoroughfare outside the Abbey grounds. The missing children weren't to be seen behind us on the drive nor immediately ahead of us. Perhaps they'd attached themselves to one of the many groups already inside the Abbey. Mr Unloss kept the nineteen remainder under threat of what would happen if any one of them had the urge to wander and I set forth to inspect children composing other school parties. Twenty minutes later, all groups in the immediate vicinity vetted, I returned to report failure.

What to do now! We were running ahead of schedule having spent less time than we'd bargained for at the Tower. We'd take the nineteen children on a mini-tour of the Abbey showing them the major points of interest such as Poets' Corner and the Tomb of the Unknown Soldier. That completed, I took the children to the grassy area of Parliament Square whilst Mr Unloss undertook a further search of the Abbey. Fortunately the weather was clement as we ate our lunches and ran off surplus energy. My thoughts were of five children lost in London and of how we would present the news to their parents. When Mr Unloss joined us, after another fruitless search, and suggested that I carry on our tour whilst he continued the hunt I declined, imagining what further calamaties might befall nineteen children and me. This, I felt, was a case of 'all for one and one for all'. As Mr Unloss returned towards the Abbey I maintained Parliament Square supervision duty.

Whilst in the midst of a boisterous game of Cowboys and Indians with me playing the part of a totem-pole, I caught a glimpse of a rather rotund London bobby approaching our group. The twinkle in his eyes was encouraging and his opening words emphasised his expression as he addressed me: 'You must be either Mr Unloss or Mrs Pilling. I've got five of your bright sparks sitting in my police car but according to their labels they should now be approaching the spot from where we picked them up over an hour ago.' Whether he said anything further I don't remember. I do remember apologising for us, the teachers, and for the children and expressing intense gratitude for the caring attitude of the London police force which has (or had) a worldwide reputation for its efficient kindness to members of the public. 'I shan't be sorry to hand them over. My gain is your loss,' commented my new found friend as he retreated to his car. I maintain in memory a clear picture of a metropolitan policeman who was a credit to his force and a source of intense relief to me and Mr Unloss.

Our absconders returned to the main party to tell their tale. After the penultimate roll-call they'd seen us queuing to cross the road and doubled back to a kerbside barrow. In the meantime we'd crossed the road and become swallowed up amid the crowds. They wandered until one of the more sensible spotted a policeman, and gave up both himself and his mates. Police were 'pigs' to our children's parents and so to the children also. They'd so enjoyed their ride in the police car and their contact with a policeman ('e were smashin') that the experience was a boost for police–children relationships. We interpreted facial expressions

*Arrival of the London Policeman
drawn by Ron Standring*

from some of those who'd missed out on the adventure and made it quite clear what would happen to any child getting lost on purpose.

We'd had our climax for that day so the prodding of the leg of the horse upholding the guard parading at Horse Guards Parade by one of our miscreants in possession of a toy bayonet was a secondary matter. Alerted by yet another of our friendly London policemen we were the only party for inspection as the Queen Mother returned to St James' Palace after an afternoon engagement. What graciousness she showed as she waved and smiled as though at a gathering of lords and ladies. For me it was a great thrill and took precedence.

No noteworthy incidents occurred during our procession to St Pancras and we were relieved to see that Holdoor, Hucknall, had again been allocated their own coach. That weariness should lull our children into a comatose condition during the hundred-mile journey to 'The Queen of the Midlands' had been our hope, but this didn't happen. With raucous voices our protégés launched into a prolonged session of 'Anything you have seen I have seen better' and with that and the sorties to the ever-attractive toilet we whiled away the hours. Parents seemed happy to have their children back and Mr Unloss and I were happy to return them. As there were no repercussions, we assumed that the travels in a police car had been played down and that's the way we preferred it to be. The following morning I entered the staff-room in time to hear Mr Unloss' reply to Miss Starbrick's 'How was the London trip?' I spent the rest of the break in a blow by blow account which enlarged upon the 'Alright, thank you' proffered by my male colleague. Other school trips, before and after, paled into insignificance when compared with THE London excursion.

CHAPTER FIFTEEN

HOLDOOR JUNIOR WAS a large school – at one time the largest junior school in Nottinghamshire. I was impressed by the way in which we (children and teachers) exercised talents for the benefit of others, people living in the neighbourhood or those who would come after us.

One male colleague gathered together nine or ten boys better known for their brawn rather than their brain. At one end of our school landscape they dug a pond. The pond was filled with water, the water with suitable plants and ferns and, in the spring, those brawny boys brought tadpoles by the dozen plus water snails, newts and numerous other pond denizens. Schoolmates tempted to approach our pond – now surrounded by shrubs – with nets and pails after school hours were foiled constantly by the brawn whilst the brain told them that if they helped to look after the pond, children coming to school in future years (maybe their own) would benefit. A little bit of mental arithmetic brings me to realise that the pond developers and the would-be raiders will now be in their late twenties and could well have children at the junior school. I wonder if they've instilled pond-pride into this new generation.

Another male colleague, a Welshman whose mother still lived in Wales, was disturbed that one type of butterfly (I think it was the Emperor) no longer lived in North Notts. During a longish holiday he would visit his mother and return with hundreds of caterpillars. His classroom was surrounded on three sides by purpose-built caterpillar cages having special ledges on which they could hang themselves to dry between cocoon and butterfly period. One summer my colleague was going on a course and, as supply teachers were at a premium, Miss Starbrick had asked me to take over. My first, in fact my only, question, was 'Are your butterflies likely to need releasing?' 'Unless the weather becomes unusually warm they'll be alright until I get back,' said my colleague. If you've read thus far you will have a good idea of what's to come. The weather became unusually warm and lessons were accompanied by cage doors clanging as beautiful butterflies exited through the French windows of the classroom. We all rushed out after the first half dozen butterflies just to make sure that they were flitting adequately and being unmolested by hereditary foes. The novelty wore off eventually and it was left to the previously elected caterpillar custodians to overlook their welfare. Some of those butterflies frequented our garden in weeks that followed. (You can recognise your own butterflies when you see them you know!) I must have been such a bore as I explained to all and sundry the important part I'd played in restoring this exquisite creature to the North of Nottinghamshire.

I've lost track of the number of times we obeyed the dictum 'Plant a tree for Britain' but I do know that if every one of the saplings flourished then, by this time, Annie Holdoor Junior School would be akin to Sleeping Beauty's palace many years after she pricked her finger.

Nottingham County Council groundsmen looked after our games fields, lawns, shrubs, trees and floral beds and kept them neat and tidy. Children, being children, often abused their industry in various ways but we were to see a change to all that. A plan to celebrate the wedding of Princess Diana and Prince Charles, in 1981, transformed our miscreants into paragons of gardening virtue. Each class was to be given rose bushes to be planted in the plot of soil immediately outside their French windows. Each teacher was given a rose bush catalogue from which, with the help of the children, the variety of rose required was to be chosen. All that was asked was that the roses should vary in colour from one soil-bed to the next thus providing variety and avoiding monotony. What a coincidence that my children chose 'Peace', my favourite. Had I influenced them or had they, under my tuition, developed a high degree of good taste? The class next door chose a pure white rose and the next but one a deep crimson so, with our blushing pink rose with gold-edged petals we were set for a harmoniously colourful summer. Once those roses began to bloom the children began their protection racket. Each day different ones were appointed to remove leaves afflicted by black-spot and dead or dying blooms. They also had to dig out weeds that were choking their roots. Suitable tools and protective gloves were provided. One day the class next door let out their tame rabbit for a breath of fresh air. Suddenly I was aware of the duty boy for the day, a belligerent lad at the best of times, hurling himself through the French windows yelling imprecations even beyond my understanding – and a mining community is a comprehensive teacher. The unfortunate bunny rabbit had chosen our spot of soil on which to conduct his (or her) toilet and was rudely disturbed and totally terrified by the tirade which assailed his ears.

The rabbit was returned to its classroom where the unsuspecting teacher was informed that if their classroom pet was found on our soil again it would be lucky to escape alive. The lad's words were lurid but sincere. Were I to repeat them this book would be a non-starter!

Miss Starbrick's twenty-fifth anniversary as Headmistress of Alice Holdoor Junior School was a cause for thanksgiving and rejoicing. A warm, sunny afternoon saw five hundred children, twenty members of staff, several ancillary workers and numerous parents gathered on the grass sward. Many gifts were presented to our Headmistress but the one that sticks in my mind was a huge cake beautifully decorated, made and presented by one of the mothers. We marvelled at Miss Starbrick's memory for names as she spoke to present pupils, past pupils – recent and long-past – and parents whose school involvement was very occasional. It was a happy informal event but made some of us realise that our well-loved Head would be obliged to retire before very long.

One morning Miss Starbrick joined us for 'break' in the staff-room and, in her self-effacing way, gave us the exciting news that she'd been invited to the prestigious Buckingham Palace Garden Party. In answering one of my questions she said 'Well, when I went before . . .'. This was the second time that she'd been honoured whilst at Alice Holdoor, on both occasions for exceptional service in the educational world. We were so proud of her and felt some of the glory reflected on us. The females wanted to know what she would be wearing on the great day. The outfit was yet to be purchased but, when it was, we had a dress rehearsal and even the males expressed enthusiastic appreciation.

We couldn't go on ignoring the prospect of Miss Starbrick's retirement much longer. There were preparations to be made and there wasn't much time left to make them. Our stage and its accoutrements were to be used to full advantage in two plays, one put on by the third- and fourth-year children and one by the first- and second-year children. We were in no doubt as to who would produce the play with the upper-school children. A very talented, attractive female drama specialist would use ideas from the children, write the sung and spoken lyrics and organise the choreography. An equally talented music specialist, the male deputy-head, would compose music to suit the words. Both of them would rehearse with the children until they had reached the highest peak of perfection possible. We had no qualms about the standard of the forthcoming upper-school play – we'd experienced their excellent quality on many previous occasions.

Who was going to supervise the play for the lower-school children? There were eight class teachers, two teachers in the deaf unit and me in special education. In previous teaching positions I'd dabbled in child dramatics but never at Annie Holdoor's so imagine my surprise and nervous trepidation when Miss Starbrick herself asked me to produce and present the lower-school play and gave me a book of fairy stories from which to glean a theme. So taken unawares was I that I had no time to find excuses – it is not a wise policy to give one's Head a downright refusal. I still wonder if I was the eleventh teacher to be asked! 'My' play was entitled 'The Dragon who liked Cake'. A very talented young lady teacher became my pianist and composer, there was excellent support from the other lower-school teachers and, perhaps the greatest relief of all, there were volunteers to make the dragon costume. Leaving the plays in rehearsal, we must turn our attention to an important event which preceded the Farewell Gathering.

The post of Headteacher of Alice Holdoor Junior had been duly advertised, interviews has been held and a short list of three males had resulted. On one auspicious day we received the exciting news that the three males would be taking part in a conducted tour of the school and would be liable to burst into any classroom without prior warning. The unwritten message was as when governors were on the prowl, 'Have your classrooms reasonably tidy, see that the children are gainfully employed and try not to be writing out your shopping list or doing your knitting.' I never found the opportunity for such personal pursuits whilst teaching juniors but well remember writing a letter home whilst in charge of a class of fourteen-year-old girls in a school in Wells when I was on teaching practice almost fifty years ago. They were quiet, slow, rural Somerset girls who, given an exercise designed to be completed in fifteen minutes would be hard-pressed to finish within the hour. At least they didn't wander from the subject as I'm doing at the present time. The only time I had a view of the three applicants was when I glanced through the classroom window as we were nearing the play-time recess. I recognised a near neighbour of ours who was already a Headmaster of a small primary school in another part of the county. The second was a man of massive proportion and the third I couldn't see at all as he was on the further side of the colossus. Most of the talk in the staff-room during break was of the three 'short listeds'. Some of the staff had had a close encounter when the men had

The Three short-listed Heads – drawn by Ron Standring

entered their classrooms and one or two had exchanged a word or two with them. Working on a process of elimination the almost unanimous opinion was that the man of great girth definitely wouldn't get this plum position. The appointment of a Head is always important but was even more so in a school that had had only one for over a quarter century and well over half its staff had never known any other Head.

As far as I'm aware, none of us lost any sleep over the question of who would be our next Headmaster. The subject occupied much of the staff-room conversation during the following day and cropped up occasionally through the following week until the day when we were summoned together, our speculation to be ended. Have you guessed the man appointed to become the Headmaster of Alice Holdoor Junior School? Right, first time! – it was the man of large girth, whose name was Mr Robins. Miss Starbrick, who must have noticed surprise registered on many faces and drainage of colour on others, gave it as her opinion that Mr Robins would be alright and was fully aware of the importance of good relationships with staff and with children. With several weeks of the summer term to go and the long end-of-year holiday to come, we turned our thoughts to preparations for the farewell activities for our retiring Head.

Through the final few weeks of the school, informal farewell events took place in classrooms and in Miss Starbrick's room as parents, ex-schoolchildren and others came to bring tokens of love and respect. This was a moving lead up to the final ceremony when our hall was crammed with children and adults, including important personages from County Hall, and we wished it was twice its size! Fond as I was, and still am, of Miss Starbrick, my mind was mainly concerned with my lower-school thespians. I remember that there were speeches from several people and various presentations and that the story was recounted of how the male members of staff, who were present, had spent an evening erecting a greenhouse in Miss Starbrick's garden.

'The Dragon who liked Cake' was wonderful. The children remembered their words, put zest into their actions and infected the audience with their natural spontaneity. The Dragon was a loveable lump who deserved his cake. I was a nervous wreck who couldn't have faced cake or anything else in that line. The upper-school play was, as predicted, 'wonderful-plus' and we hoped Miss Starbrick knew that we'd pulled out all the stops mainly for her benefit.

It's true to say that all retirements bring rosy-hued speeches and that the person retiring is made to appear a paragon of virtue but the love and respectful admiration felt for Miss Starbrick were clearly evident. Our traditional end-of-term extravaganza of cream cakes and cups of tea in the staff-room brought more informal speeches while many voices were wavery and not a few eyes wet. As she left, amidst a welter of good wishes, our Headmistress of twenty-five years exorted us to believe that her replacement would prove to be a man of fine quality who would make his way gently and with sensitivity. On that note of reassurance, we left to enjoy our much anticipated lengthy holiday.

CHAPTER SIXTEEN

THIS CHAPTER OF my book has been delayed for several years so that the Head involved might be well away from this area after a retirement that received not so much as a notice in the local press, let alone an article! From my fascination with words, crosswords in particular, I knew the meaning of 'enigma'. I was about to meet one!

On that first morning of the autumn term, 1978, twenty-two teachers arrived in school scrubbed and polished at least a quarter of an hour before the bell was rung when eager children would rush in. Cancel the last phrase – our children never rushed in but entered school in a quiet and dignified manner! The teachers were present and the children also, but the Headmaster was conspicuous by his absence. Our Deputy Head (whom most of us would have welcomed as our Head) conducted morning assembly during which those of us fortunate enough to be facing the windows overlooking the car park, saw a large, opulent limousine purr into the space reserved for the Head-teacher. As the driver emerged, one could fully understand why the car was large. Mr Robins was, without a doubt, the largest man I'd ever seen and, as he walked to the front door of the school, anyone blessed with imagination could see the light fading and feel the foundations quivering. One should not dislike or despise a man, or a woman, for being grossly overweight. Cyril Smith, the one time MP for Rochdale, was almost as fat as Mr Robins and he was well liked and respected. We mustn't judge our new Head on the size of his diaphragm. Some of us know, from painful personal experience, the dastardly effect of certain medications. So I waited, along with my colleagues, to meet this man into whose charge we had been given. We waited in vain for the only person he met that day was the school secretary who was evidently so busy typing for him that she was unable to come to the staff-room to give us the 'low down'.

The second morning saw a different limousine draw into the space reserved for the Head-teacher. Again it was large and opulent but of a different colour. It was driven into position with five minutes to spare before the school bell sounded. This information was delivered by a member of staff whose classroom was in the fairly close vicinity of the Head's room. Those of us mainly concerned with first- and second-year children were further away and so relied upon colleagues teaching third- and fourth-years.

Teachers and children assembled in the Hall. The silence, unusual and almost unbearable, was shattered by heavy, ponderous footsteps slowly proceeding along the approach-corridor to the hall. How were the children about to react? Would there be nudging and tittering? What about the child upon whom my eyes were fixed at that moment who was prone to vocalise his opinions very audibly? Would Mr Robins understand if I were to gag the potential offender with his scruffy pullover and then practise my half-Nelson upon him? Children are so unpredictable – not a titter, not a nudge, not a vocal rendition but wide open eyes, in some cases wide open mouths and, in all cases, the appearance of a hypnotic state. What Mr Robins said to the children I can't remember except for something that came just before he left the Hall. As he had motored along the road to our school that morning he'd passed one or two children who looked as though they were going to be late. 'It is never good to be be late,' he said. I decided, at the time, that he was being facetious and directing his remark against himself. But, in retrospect, I believe it was my first experience of his enigmatic nature.

Mr Robins joined us in the staff-room for the morning break which, in the Infant and Junior School, was more commonly known as playtime. Our staff-room, whilst furbished in a superior manner to other staff-rooms I have known, did not sport a surplus of easy chairs but, on the appearance of Mr Robins, our widest and firmest chair was made available – (two of us would normally occupy it during staff meetings!). With our Head seated, if overlapping, we felt less diminutive. Few of us had realised that his height was only a little less awesome than his width and that, when standing, he couldn't help but look down on us. The atmosphere was a little strained, to say the least, but, if not a fully relaxed playtime, it proved a friendly and informative one. We learnt that Mr Robins lived in a city some thirty miles south of the school and that either of his cars could make the journey in twenty minutes travelling north along the M1. None of us suggested that the 70 mph limit was being broken or that leaving home earlier would prevent a late arrival at school or even that one car would be sufficient. We were all eminently circumspect.

Later in the week, when I was thoroughly involved in some educational exercise with my group of children, a fourth-year child came into our room and delivered a note from Mr Robins. He was conducting a sale and, as all goods had to go before the end of the day, would I present myself forthwith. This was intriguing and, loth as I was to desert my field of duty, I picked up my handbag and set forth to fulfil my Headmaster's request. My knock having received a booming 'Come', I went into a room full of aromatic cigar smoke and, with some difficulty, picked out Mr Robins sitting behind a desk almost completely covered by a baffling variety of articles. 'Help yourself to what you like,' said the stallholder, 'it's what that silly woman left, taking up space in my cupboards.' Little did he know how much his entirely faulty description of Miss Starbrick had diminished him in my opinion. I can only suppose that the articles in question had been given to Miss Starbrick by pupils and, being too numerous to be given house-room, had been secreted in her cupboard away from peeping eyes. I think it was a sardonic grunt that I got from the new Head when I delivered my possible explanation. Thinking that the least I could do was to offer a receptive home to some of the goods, I chose a rather attractive barometer and several equally attractive table-mats. Seventeen years later, the barometer hangs on a wall of our porch and has given great delight to visiting grandsons who have predicted the weather with fair accuracy. The table-mats are reduced in number, through long and faithful service, but two remain to perform continuing daily duty. Reverting to the day I acquired them, I should point out that I didn't buy them for, when I began to forage for my purse, Mr Robins explained that he wasn't aiming to support any charity, just getting rid of clutter. You'll be happy to learn that, when I returned to my classroom, each child was gainfully employed, so much so that the thought of leaving them more often sprang to my mind!

Our initial reaction to our new Head was not good, neither was it improved by news from our Senior Mistress. Evidently she had been socialising over the weekend with friends and acquaintances from a wide area of the county and beyond. I'm not sure now whether it was between the pâté de fois gras and the smoked salmon or the thick vegetable soup and the spotted dick that one of the company had waved his or her cocktail stick as a means of attracting her attention and then spoken. It was a long story – so long that we'd barely arrived at the After Eight mints before the bell summoned us to the classroom from the staff-room. I, never at my best when attempting to précis, will, nevertheless, endeavour to condense the Senior Mistress's story whilst capturing the salient points. One of the guests had a sister who had a friend who knew someone whose sister taught in a school in that area. The fifth person in that august chain of females had taught in the school from which Mr Robins had so recently moved and, according to several word-of-mouth stories, every member of staff had been glad to see the back of him. Whether he'd been the Deputy Head or the Head I didn't gather and I was unwilling to ask for a repeat of the story. To those of my colleagues who asked my opinion (there were always quite a few – on account of my matronly middle age or my being the wife of a Parson?) I suggested that we should give Mr Robins the benefit of the doubt and wait and see how he acquitted himself at Alice Holdoor Junior School.

When Miss Starbrick came to see us, after half-term and to collect some things she'd left (I hoped they didn't include a barometer and several place-mats), all wished she were back and some even voiced their thoughts. She assured us again that we'd be alright with Mr Robins if we gave him enough time to find his feet. We didn't mention his late arrivals, which continued, as she had always arrived in time to be in her room at least a quarter of an hour before school commenced, thus having time to see any parent, child or teacher who needed to speak with her.

Having decided that my reminiscences concerning Mr Robins are having a depressing effect upon me, I surmise that readers are suffering a similar debilitation. I, therefore, propose to devote this paragraph to the good points in our Head's favour. During the penultimate week of the autumn term, a week or two before Christmas, a magnificent tin of Quality Street chocolates appeared in the staff-room. Each of us always brought a treat for the rest of the staff when it was our birthday – it always seemed the wrong way round to me. We couldn't recall any member of staff having a birthday so near to Christmas or anyone who would bring so large a tin! There was speculation that the tin was empty but when one of our well-built males had considerable difficulty in raising it from the floor it was obvious that this was not the case. Was it full of some sort of waste material? The sealed tape with which it was securely bound ruled out that possibility. Mouths watering, we left it but when we came back to the staff-room at playtime an amusing note, fastened to the alluring tin, announced it to be a Christmas present from Mr Robins to his staff. We appreciated his kind generosity although members who spent longer in the staff-room than others started to get more than their fair share. Like the well-mannered, extremely properly brought-up creatures that we were, we offered our thanks and appreciation to our benefactor even offering a chocolate, if not two! Twenty-two adults, turned loose on delectable confectionery can speedily reduce the quantity – and we did. It wasn't long before the weakest female was able to lift the tin with ease. To our amazement, by the time our first tin was down to its last few contents, another unopened tin of equally majestic proportion arrived to take its place. The same thoughtful and generous action took place each Christmas time whilst I remained at Annie Holdoor and, no doubt, continued after I left.

Those readers (if any remain) who are employed in industry may be wondering why there was so much excitement about two large tins of chocolates shared among twenty-two when *their* Christmas bonus is twice that value per employee! A teacher receives no perks from employer at Christmas or at any other time of the year, at least not in my experience. I seem to hear the comment: 'I should think not! You do five hours a day, have at least ten weeks holiday in a year, get a terrific salary and then want perks.'

In the last paragraph I made mention of an amusing note written by Mr Robins. Our Head had a ready wit and a good sense of humour. Humour and wit are almost alike in meaning, according to the dictionary, but both are referred to as qualities. As far as I'm concerned a quality is something that's good, wholesome and valuable. It must be said, if this is to be a fair trial, that for most of the time Mr Robins' humour and wit were laudable but it was the least of the time that concerned me. So suddenly that it was hardly noticeable, the humour became maliciously barbed and the wit, warped. We would find ourselves laughing at the expense of some person for whom we had a high regard. Perhaps a little jealousy, on my part, coloured my feelings on his written manifestation of wit. Until Mr Robins arrived at Alice Holdoor, I was the one responsible for sending amusing notes from classroom to classroom. Now, I had to admit, the Headmaster's notes were on a higher plane of wit than mine. The enigma showed itself yet again as, in the midst of thanks for his latest piece of written wit we were pulled up short by being asked why we had not responded to his request. From that time forth, we were never sure how to treat his notes. If we took them seriously we were laughed at but, if we didn't, we faced sarcastic chiding. Their arrival became a hazard rather than a pleasure.

I explained earlier that I was among those situated farthest from the Head's room and therefore our news was almost always second-hand. Some of the items I took with a pinch of salt (a strange expression!) feeling them to have been lavishly embroidered, but when an earnest young male teacher asked me if I'd heard that Mr Robins was giving away stationery, art supplies and sports equipment to other schools in the area, I decided to seek the truth from the horse's mouth. Loud laughter and 'Would I do a thing like that?' was the response but it was true that our stockrooms were less well stocked than previously and that schools in the area had received a boost. I'm not for a moment suggesting that our Head had taken money from the transaction. He had a wife who was a Deputy Headmistress, he told us that he was a shareholder in some very profitable businesses and that he was a prolific writer of books and had publishers in Holland. If the transference of stock was of his doing, then I would think it to have been to ingratiate himself and attract attention.

Mr Robins continued to be late for school on most days of the week. Sometimes he wouldn't arrive at all and, on other occasions, he came in for the afternoon session. We never knew what had kept him away. The school ran just as well without him, staff preferred it and the children didn't seem to notice. He didn't see them as individuals, just *en masse*. He was usually on time on a Friday because that was the day when he took Assembly. I invariably enjoyed his Assembly. He had a commanding presence and captured the attention of his audience immediately. The stories he told were gripping, whether true or fiction, and the morals came over so naturally, needing no emphasis. Here again is the enigma. Had you known nothing of the man you would have thought that here was the ideal Headmaster for a junior school. Knowing him, you were aware that most of the worthy morals were absent from his own character and he was urging the children to do what he said and not what he did.

Providing one is not engaged on dinner duty there is no compulsion for a teacher to remain on school premises during the dinner-hour. It was not for us to question where our Headmaster went or with whom but I learnt the information from an acquaintance of mine who was the Headmaster of a much smaller school in the town. He'd had the Area Education Officer in his school and, during conversation, the latter had mentioned that he'd come to know Mr Robins well through sharing meals with him on several occasions. Our Head was booking a table at a prestigious restaurant and inviting the top notch of the county educational world to break bread with him. Very generous of our Mr Robins and very conducive to his educational welfare but not the sort of thing to further his image in the eyes of his counterparts in the town's schools.

I could go on giving examples of our enigmatic Head's idiosyncrasies but I won't. Alice Holdoor was not as happy a school as before. When I heard that Nottinghamshire Education Council was prepared to accept requests for early retirement I decided to make one. I had several valid reasons for wishing to finish my teaching career but I didn't give the main one! During the next two years, several of my colleagues left Alice Holdoor, not for retirement but for a change of post. The stalwarts who stayed have been able to appreciate the enthusiasm and peace of mind that has come with a dedicated and sympathetic Head. Alice Holdoor is happy and riding high.

During the past decade, the state of disquiet within our state educational system has led to teachers fleeing the profession much as rats are purported to flee the sinking ship. The former I know from personal experience, the latter I have never witnessed.

It may be that, among our readers, we have aspiring teachers and some who are already training. To those of you coming under the aforementioned categories I say, 'Put your aspirations into concrete terms. Put your whole self into your training. Then, aspirers, trainers and trained, carry on teaching with all your heart, soul, might and main.' My experiences are, on the whole, removed from the norm, hence the title of this book. In spite of them and, in some cases, because of them, I enjoyed my twenty-five years of teaching and still enjoy being accosted by former pupils – they've changed beyond all recognition from eight-year-olds to twenty-eight-year-olds whereas my change is from brown hair to mainly white hair and from unbespectacled to always bespectacled except in sleep! They invariably commence by saying 'Do you remember when . . .?' I always do, because that's what they want me to do. Love your children, not in a soppy sort of way but by being concerned for their all-round welfare. Be able to stand where they stand and think as they think and, when you understand them and have established a rapport with them you may begin to teach them with a degree of success. As for Head-teachers! The majority of them are genuinely concerned about their staff and the children. I was unfortunate with one or two of mine but very happy with the others. Do as they say, remembering that they have been vested with authority, but if their orders smack of despotism then, quietly and courteously, question them, although never in the hearing of children or other teachers.

Those of us who are ex-teachers enjoy the freedom from stress and strain but miss being involved in school situations. We're still very much concerned with the education of children and need to soft-pedal with our grandchildren. We teachers of yesteryear look to the teachers of today and tomorrow to produce the type of experiences that everyone will believe and be glad to believe.